VARLA VENTURA'S

PARANORMAL PARLOR

M000222842

VARLA VENTURA'S

PARANORMAL PARLOR

Ghosts, Séances & Tales of True Hauntings

VARLA VENTURA

WEISER BOOKS

This edition first published in 2018 by Weiser Books, an imprint of
Red Wheel/Weiser, LLC
With offices at:
65 Parker Street, Suite 7
Newburyport, MA 01950
www.redwheelweiser.com

Copyright © 2018 by Varla Ventura

All rights reserved. No part of this publication may be reproduced or transmitted in any form or by any means, electronic or mechanical, including photo-
copying, recording, or by any information storage and retrieval system, without
permission in writing from Red Wheel/Weiser, LLC. Reviewers may quote brief
passages.

ISBN: 978-1-57863-633-4

Library of Congress Cataloging-in-Publication Data available upon request.

Cover art adapted from a promotional poster for American magician Harry
Kellar by the Strobridge Lithographic Co., Cincinnati, New York, ca. 1894.
From the Performing Arts Poster Collection at the Library of Congress.

Interior by Deborah Dutton
Typeset in Palatino LT Std

Printed in Canada
MAR
10 9 8 7 6 5 4 3 2 1

*For Dina
my sister in blood
and in horror*

I will tell you that strange happening just as it took place, with no attempt to explain it. Unless I went mad for one short hour it must be explainable, though. Yet I was not mad, and I will prove it to you. Imagine what you will.

—GUY DE MAUPASSANT, *A GHOST*

Contents

Terrifyingly True Tales of Ghostly Encounters Including Child Ghosts, Things That Moan in the Woods, Warning Ghosts, Friendly Ghosts, and the Curious Case of the Haunted Toothbrush

Haunted Places and the Ghosts That Love Them; Haunted Houses, Hotels, Hospitals, Cemeteries, and the Empire of the Dead

Introduction

What Fools We Mortals Be

As I write these words, a sudden storm has come upon us, thunderclouds thickening the sky so that, in spite of the daylight hour, it appears dark. So dark, in fact, that the only lights in my room are flashes of lightning. It is a storm like those that horror writers conjure up to set the mood for haunted entrapment, the kind that keeps you locked inside your home in the company of ghosts.

For most of my life I have found the company of ghosts to be of comfort. Perhaps I am lucky that I have not been pursued by a scratching, loathsome poltergeist or made to feel that I cannot breathe by a desperate specter. And maybe luck has nothing to do with it:

maybe these experiences are just around the paranormal corner, waiting patiently for their turn to have me in the night. In this book I recount some of my own experiences along with encounters experienced by those I hold near and dear. You'll also find places to seek your own ghosts, from cemeteries to destitute institutions. And you'll learn the fascinating stories behind some of the most elaborate psychic salons of the day, during the late Victorian craze of communication with the afterlife.

I suppose you might say that I talk to dead people. Or rather, sometimes they talk to me. I am no professional psychic; I do not lay claim to the second sight and can't predict your future nor offer advice in the present. However, I've had enough encounters to say I wouldn't be out of place at a dead man's party. When it comes to dreams, the dead pay regular visits. I am certain it is not a rare talent, but many nights I am visited by family and friends who have gone to the Great Beyond. Often, they carry messages. These messages always make perfect sense in the dream, but in the light of day frequently befuddle. The trick is to write the message down and recite it, just as clearly as they told you. It may not mean a thing to you, but it might make sense to the person you deliver it to.

"'Twas just a dream." We use these words to soothe a frightened child in the night who is sure a monster is lurking inside the closet, just out of reach of the light. We use them to convince ourselves that the eerie feeling we have that something isn't right is just a dream we can't explain. But dreams are powerful tools: whether they are prophetic warnings (get out of town, now!) or messages that allow us to question our actions in the waking world, there's no denying that we've all had a dream or two that has made us think twice.

I can remember the first time I learned lucid dreaming (though admittedly my talents went downhill and now I must work harder to make it happen). I had a terrible nightmare and woke up crying for my mother. When she came to comfort me, she did not actually say to me, "It's only a dream. Go back to sleep." Instead, she asked me what I had dreamed. When I told her I dreamed I was running in a field and I fell into a large hole that I could not get out of, she offered me this solution: "Go back to sleep and have that dream again. But this time, when you fall in the hole, picture Sir Dog (our family Great Dane) appearing with a rope that he drops down to you and pulls you out." And so I did just that. I fell asleep, dreamed the dream, fell in the hole, and was rescued. I was four years old.

While ghosts might frighten some, I dare say if you've read this far, you're not the type to easily cringe. If you are easily scared, I can't assure you that nothing will happen. All I can say is leave the light on. It may flicker, it may even briefly go out—but it almost always comes right back on again.

In loving freakitude,
Varla Ventura
North Woods, 2018

Chapter 1

Under Paranormal Circumstances

*Terrifyingly True Tales of Ghostly Encounters
Including Child Ghosts, Things That Moan
in the Woods, Warning Ghosts, Friendly
Ghosts, and the Curious Case of the
Haunted Toothbrush*

Creatures of mist, half credited;
Our faint form flings
No shadow in moonlight on the bed
We visit; noiseless is our tread,
Who come from deserts of the dead,
Where no bird sings.

—ANON, *GHOST STORIES AND PRESENTIMENTS*

Here There Be Ghosts

I have never met a ghost story I didn't like. Whether it ends in a ridiculous joke (the wrapping paper in the closet the source of the phantom *rap, rap, rapping*) or lingers long enough to make you jump at shadows, I find the genre and all of its many incantations delightful. But nothing quite gets me going like the story right from the mouths of babes: when a firsthand experience is recounted to me—preferably in the dim light of the fire on a dark and stormy night. When I began writing this book, I put out a call for stories among my people: the midnight podcaster, the horror novelist, the paranormal lovers, and those whom the paranormal seem to love. While my original intention was to create one opening chapter chock-full of as-told-to-me tales, as I gathered the tales, they found their own way into the manuscript. In later chapters, you'll find the case of the haunted tarot deck and the pot-smoking Ouija board user and even a haunting from the catacombs of Paris. In this chapter, among the many stories I wanted to tell from my own experiences was one about the child ghost I lived with for a number of years. Turns out, I wasn't the only one with a kid apparition. In addition, you will find the unnamed Lovecraftian thing that moaned in the woods and other horrifying joys. Read on, my friends, read on.

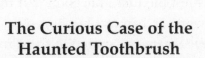

The Curious Case of the Haunted Toothbrush

Just a few short years ago, I was lucky enough to be blessed with a little changeling of my own: I brought my own wee babe home to our Victorian flat in San Francisco and he spent many happy years learning to crawl, walk, and read among the rattling windows and resident ghosts. It should not surprise my readers that

the introduction of a little one into a household actually marked an increase in paranormal activity—albeit of the gentlest kind. However, having my own child around was not the first indication that the ghost was friendly toward or perhaps fascinated by children. In fact, we never were certain if the ghost was that of a child, a caretaker or nanny, or simply just a kindhearted and shy spirit who felt comfortable with kids.

The incident with the toothbrush occurred some years earlier. My mother, my sister, and her three children were visiting us over one long weekend. Both of my nieces were in the spare bedroom (what would later become the nursery), and this room was directly across from the bathroom. At the time, the elder niece was only about eight years old. After a day of exploring the park and sights of San Francisco, we settled in for the evening. When bedtime came, each of the three kiddos brushed their teeth diligently, using their favorite electric toothbrushes, and then set them up, one by one, like little soldiers along the back of the tiny sink. Eventually we all went to bed.

Sometime in the night my niece woke up to the sound of her toothbrush going on. Nonplussed, she got up and switched it off and then climbed back into bed. Before she could pull the covers back up over her, the toothbrush went on again. This time, Grandma, who was also in the room, heard it. With a little encouragement from Grandma, my niece again got up to turn the toothbrush off. Then she crept back to bed. No sooner had she returned to the room than the toothbrush went off again! Wide-eyed, she bravely retrieved it, but this time she marched it to the kitchen,

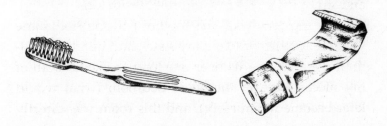

where she shut it off and set it on the windowsill. At this point, I also heard the toothbrush and wondered what on earth my niece was doing with her toothbrush in the night, especially walking around the apartment with it. When I got up, she told me that she had turned it off three times, but the toothbrush kept coming back on, so she put it in the kitchen to keep it quiet. And it worked!

When we were readying the apartment a few years later for the birth of the Baby Ventura, we discovered beneath the layers of paint a child's wallpaper depicting a 1930s-era circus scene. I suppose it makes great sense that the paranormal activity continued, generally revolving around that room or relating to children in the house.

There was the time when I came home close to midnight, my sleeping baby in my arms, having just returned from a long road trip. I opened the door to the apartment and switched a dim side lamp on (don't wake a sleeping babe) when I had the feeling I was not alone—and I am not referring to my exhausted child. I looked around from my vantage point by the door and from where I stood in the hallway could see into both bedrooms. There, standing near the foot of the crib, seemed to be a small figure—lumpy, hazy, possibly childlike, and gone within seconds. I was not afraid, but certainly surprised. The lamp flickered a few times. I did not approach the crib with my tiny one, but rather snuggled him into a bassinet in the living room while I inspected the house. I discovered nothing. I should note that my cat, Midnight, was not around, as dear friends of ours were watching His Fuzziness while I traveled.

One morning, a rather dark and gloomy (in the finest way possible) morning, I was awake and preparing something very pure and pureed for the Baby Ventura. He was gleefully playing in his little activity center near me in the kitchen, when I heard the sound of one of his toys being jingled from the next room. My first thought was casual—I had grown used to hearing the baby shake toys and rattles while I was dashing into the kitchen to check the progress of the sugar skulls or

pumpkin stew. But in the seconds that followed, I realized that the baby was next to me, and that nothing at his chubby little fingertips was able to make that sound. As I was looking over at him to see if he'd snuck a little rattle in with him, I heard it again. This time it was unmistakable. It was the sound of

a toy being rattled, something with a little bell, and it was definitely coming from the other room. There was no one else in the apartment, no cat (Midnight had passed away and I had not yet adopted his successor), no open windows, no water dripping or laundry whirring. It was just me, the baby, and something rattling a little toy. I froze, looking at the baby (can babies detect ghosts the way dogs and cats do?), and felt some major chills rippling down my spine. I carefully looked into the living room, where nothing seemed out of place. I stared down the hall, where some toys were strewn about. Now even a freak like me gets scared if her baby is threatened, but I oh-so-bravely made my way into the other room to see if I could explain it. Was there a toy that had fallen? A jingle I could replicate? Nothing. I could not even trace the source of the sound. I crept down the hall toward the nursery and did a check there. Nothing. To be honest, I had expected to see some errant human sneaking in from the other rooftop on the lam. But there was nothing—nothing paranormal and nothing abnormal. All windows and doors were locked, and all became

> **It was just me, the baby, and something rattling a little toy.**

calm and bright as the sun finally peeked through the San Francisco fog.

On stormy nights, when the moon shines faintly through the fleeting clouds, she stalks of gigantic stature with death-like aspect, and black, hollow eyes, wrapt in grave clothes which float in the wind, and stretches her immense arm over the solitary hut, uttering lamentable cries in the tempestuous darkness.

—ELLIOTT O'DONNELL, *THE BANSHEE*

Baby on Board

Was it a child ghost or a ghost that likes children? I'll never know for sure. But I certainly understood when Hunter Shea generously offered to share this true story of the spirit in his house, whom he and his family affectionately call the Boy Boarder.

Hunter Shea is truly a man after my own heart, the product of a misspent childhood watching scary movies, reading forbidden books, and wishing Bigfoot would walk past his house. He doesn't just write about the paranormal—he actively seeks out the things that scare the hell out of people and experiences them for himself. Hunter's novels can even be found on display at the International Cryptozoology Museum. *The Montauk Monster* was named one of the best reads of the summer by *Publishers Weekly*. Not since Dr. Frankenstein has someone been as dedicated to making monsters, penning such titles as *The Jersey Devil*, *Loch Ness Revenge*, *They Rise*, *Swamp Monster Massacre*, and *The Dover Demon*. His latest book, *We Are Always Watching*, is terrifying readers around the globe. His video podcast *Monster Men* is one of the most-watched horror podcasts in the world. Living with his wonderful family and two cats, he's happy to be close enough to New York City to gobble down Gray's Papaya hot dogs

when the craving hits. You can follow his madness at *www.huntershea.com*.

A Comforting Ghost

We live in a two-family house in the suburbs of New York. We moved in here in 1993. At the time, we'd been married about a year and my wife had been sick a lot. She had a muscle disorder, but now she was experiencing constant stomachaches and a fever, and she couldn't eat. By the time we moved into the house, she was so sick we ended up having to rush her to the hospital. She was twenty-three years old, losing weight rapidly, and over the course of a year of doctor's visits we still had no diagnosis for what was wrong with her. Eventually a doctor did exploratory surgery and discovered that her stomach was actually full of gangrene. The anti-inflammatory medication she was on to help her muscle disorder had caused a rupture, and her body was poisoning itself. She was hospitalized with a 5 percent chance of survival. She spent 1993–95 in and out of the hospital and on 24/7 life support.

Gradually, she got stronger, and I was able to bring her home from the hospital. She still was very sick and was typically only awake about an hour a day. I had a full-time job that I had to go to each day in order to try to pay our mounting medical bills, and I hated leaving her. The stress was something I can't even describe, and I have no idea how I actually handled it at the time. I was in my early twenties and did not have the tools to cope with everything. But somehow, we did it.

One day, I was in the kitchen doing dishes when I saw something out of the corner of my eye. I turned to see a little boy in my hallway. He was about eight or nine years old. My first thought was that it was a neighborhood kid, but I didn't understand how he could have gotten into the hallway without coming in the door right off the kitchen, where I was. I was pretty freaked out (not because I thought this was a ghost, but because I was wondering how the heck this kid got in my house) and called out to him. He suddenly turned and walked down the hallway toward my wife's room. I immediately followed him, but even at this point I didn't consider that I was following a ghost. I was concerned that this kid was going into her room, where there were a ton of wires and cords that he could trip on and unplug, harming my wife. Her room wasn't far away, only like six feet or so, and I rushed inside. He wasn't there. I checked the windows. They were all closed and we were on  the second floor. I knew the boy didn't just jump out. My wife was asleep, the machines were humming. I sat on the edge of her bed, completely perplexed.

I told no one about this. Everyone we knew was already very concerned about us, and I was young, so I didn't know how to ask for help. The last thing I wanted was anyone thinking that I was "losing it" and not able to care for my wife. So I kept the incident to myself. And I didn't think much more about it, as I had more pressing matters to attend to.

A few weeks later, I saw him again. He walked out of the kitchen and into the living room and headed again toward the room where my wife was sleeping. I started to wonder if this was a ghost, but I was not afraid. Keep in mind this was the 1990s, and there weren't all the ghost shows and paranormal investigations like there are today. The third time I saw him, I decided to explore more about the history of the house. I was starting to wonder if this was the spirit of someone who'd passed there, so I started asking the neighbors who had lived in the area the longest. One of our neighbors had lived there for nearly sixty years, and had never heard of any child who had died in the house or on our block. However, our house was seventy years old at the time we bought it, and for the first thirty years, it was the only one in the area. Still, I found no history of death, and no one had ever heard of any children passing away there.

Over the course of the year, I saw him about seven more times. And each time I did not feel afraid, but rather felt an emotional peace. This was at a time when there was no peace for me. Each time I would see him I would get up, follow him to the bedroom where my wife was, and of course he would never be there. I still never told anyone, most especially her.

A year later, my wife had recovered enough to be taken off life support. I told her how much I hated when I left for work, because I was worried that she was alone and scared. Now that she was feeling better I felt less terrible when I left.

And she said, "You know, when I was really sick, I have to tell you, there were times when you left and I felt comforted. I used to see this little boy. He came into the room and sat on the bed." She then went on to describe the same child I had seen. A boy of eight or nine years old, in a plain T-shirt and pants with short hair. So I finally told her that I had seen him and often felt that someone was there.

We never believed in angels, and for years we really didn't talk much about it. Her mother had told us that she had given birth to two stillborn sons and she wondered if this was one of them looking over my wife. We didn't know if this was a ghost, a guardian, what. He stopped appearing around 1995, and we didn't see him again until 2000, when my wife was diagnosed with cervical cancer shortly after finding out she was pregnant. She gave birth to our daughter and then underwent treatment. He appeared again. I would tell her I'd seen him, and she'd describe when he appeared to her. We called him the Boy Boarder. It seems like he comes around when she is sick. In 2006, she was diagnosed with a heart issue. I didn't see him so much as I was seeing flashes of light, but she was still seeing him. We've come to simply accept him.

We don't know what he is. A spirit? Her brother? An angel? Our collective unconscious conjuring him up when we need him? Our daughters have both seen him, and my wife sees him often. We've never done any EVP recordings or investigations. We all agree that he's part of our lives. It's weird to describe it that way, but it's true. It's like he's part of our family.

—HUNTER SHEA, AS TOLD TO VARLA VENTURA

"In every real man a child is hidden that wants to play."

—FRIEDRICH NIETZSCHE

We Are Family

The idea of family ghosts, or ghosts that attach themselves to people and are "inherited" from generation to generation, can perhaps be traced back to a time when families remained in one place for longer. Were these "inherited" ghosts simply ghosts of a place, a castle for example, where all of the bloodline was destined to live? The Irish banshee is sometimes equated with a family ghost, as at one time this supernatural songstress was said to belong to the original clans of Ireland from which all Irish bloodlines are descended. In Germany, we find the White Lady, a warning phantasm associated—like the banshee—with those of ancient lineage. She warns her mortal family of impending death and is not attached to place so much as person, as she will follow the descendants from town to town. In Austria, a White Woman appears howling on rooftops to warn families that someone in the house below will die within the month. And in Italy there are numerous examples of "inherited" spirits, especially among prominent families of royal lineage. In Venice, for example, the Donati possess a ghost in the form of a disembodied head that floats into the doorway of a doomed family member. But are these ghosts attached to a family, or is it that the

ability to see them—the second sight, the Shining, the clairvoyance—is actually what is inherited? Either way, ghosts are no doubt in our DNA.

In his book *Witchcraft and Superstitious Record in the South-Western District of Scotland*, J. Maxwell Wood records this story of a family ghost that seems to provide some relief to those who are dying:

In the Lowlands of Scotland stood an old manor house, where the owner's wife was on her death-bed. The ancient furniture still remained in the room, so the invalid lay in a four-post bed, with curtains all round it, wherein many generations of the family had been born and died. The curtains were drawn at its foot and on the side nearest the wall, but they were open on the other to a blazing fire, before which sat an attendant nurse. A tall screen on her left hand shielded her from the draught from a door, whose top was visible above it; and as the nurse sat there she became conscious that the door was opening and that a hand seemed to rest for a moment on the top of the screen. Presently, as she watched, half-paralysed with fear, a figure appeared from behind the screen—the figure of a young woman clothed in a sacque of rich brocade, over a pink silk petticoat, and wearing a head-dress of the time of Queen Anne. This figure advanced with a gentle undulating movement to the bed and bent down over it. Then the nurse jumped up and stretched out her hand to the bell-pull; and, lo! when she looked again the figure had vanished, and her patient lay there dead, with an expression of rapturous content on her sunken face.

Later, when the last sad rites had been accomplished, this nurse wandered into the picture gallery in company with the

housekeeper, and pausing before a certain portrait, exclaimed that there was the original of the unknown lady.

"Ah," came the answer, "that lady lived here when Queen Anne was on the throne. They say she had a sad life with her lord, and died young. Ever since she is believed, when the mistress of the manor dies, to appear beside the bed, and—and"——

"You need not tell me more," said the nurse, "for I also have seen her."

South by Southwest

If the road is dusty and your truck is rusty
You've found your way to Santa Fe.

—PERINE PARKER, "KEEP DRIVING"

Alix Benedict is a writer, artist, and confectioner who has had paranormal encounters throughout her life. In *The Book of the Bizarre*, she shared her haunting story of being alone in a basement when she felt her hair being pulled and was able to see—in the reflection of the window— her hair standing up, but no person there pulling on it. As a kid, she lived on a sailboat (her

mother recalls a specific night when they heard mermaids chanting) as well as in numerous haunted homes. Her story of the Santa Fe Kid is among the most vivid of her experiences, and she shares it here with you, dear reader, for the first time in print.

The Santa Fe Kid

A most significant haunting in my life took place circa 1990 on Kathryn Avenue, a quiet side street of Santa Fe, New Mexico, in a tiny, windowless shotgun house. A shotgun house, common in Santa Fe, is the style of home with a long, narrow footprint, where the rooms are arranged one after another, which means you pass through each room to the next—there is no hallway. There were no exterior windows at all and the space itself was long and skinny. It was the original house on the land—next door a sprawling adobe home had been built and was occupied by my landlord. The old house had been converted into an in-law and was rented to me.

> **In the morning I'd wake to my sugar bowl upside down on the Formica kitchen table. Miraculously, not a grain of sugar could be found outside the bowl. Not a one.**

At twenty-three, I was quite the socializer and drinker—bartending and waitressing in the plaza and hardly at home but for sleep and showering. But I had not been there long when I noticed something strange: in the morning I'd wake to my sugar bowl upside down on the Formica kitchen table. Miraculously, not a grain of sugar could be found outside the bowl. Not a one.

Each morning I would release the sugar, swipe it back into the bowl, and replace it in its proper place upright. Over time, the unused and abused sugar ambered, adopted flecks and bits.

The second thing that got my attention was waking, chilly, around 4 a.m. with no top sheet, no covers in sight. I'd find that I'd strewn them about, always my Mickey Mouse blanket missing from my bed. They would not be in the room around me, nor in the next room, but straight through to the dining room. (Remember, the shotgun house has rooms in a row and open to one another.) This was probably the first event that was happening, but I'd convinced myself I somehow was sleepily dragging the blankets myself on the way to the loo. This occurred nightly.

The third thing took me a few weeks to notice 'cause I didn't often use the front room, the living room. But one night I was in there and was struck by white lights sweeping along the walls and the ceiling. I attributed them to headlights of cars pulling in and out of driveways opposite me until I reminded myself that there were no windows in the house! The front door was always closed, as there was no screen. Friends were able to catch video of the streaking lights during one of my ghostly slumbovers that last month there.

The fourth thing that really did the trick was the missing soap bars. Too often I'd find the soap bars in my shower and bathroom sink were missing. Gone. Drove me nuts. One day, I was tippy-toed atop a chair cleaning the highest shelf in the pantry and felt twenty-plus lumps. Soap bars, a variety of sizes, were stuck to the liner on the uppermost shelf—lumps as far as I could reach, all the way back to the wall.

That day I was certain I was being haunted.

Other strange occurrences included random placement of marbles—I'd go to put my shoes on and find a marble in my shoe. I'd also sometimes hear what sounded like rolling marbles across the kitchen floor, marbles hitting things. Also my radio would never work and would go on and off at random times, especially at five in the morning.

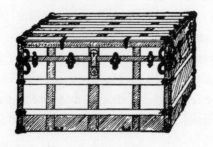

I was delighted. My landlords were not. Being devout Catholics, they were horrified. They accused me of witchcraft, claiming a pentagram sticker on my steamer trunk was proof enough I'd either brought it with me or conjured it up. They never once disputed any incidents but were both decidedly set against hearing any more particulars or talking about it at all. They wanted me gone within forty-eight hours. I was flabbergasted when I couldn't reason with them. I slept at a friend's house, then returned the next day to pack and move, opening the front door to discover a priest in my living room, muttering.

Luckily a kindly neighbor let me store my larger items in her garage while I couch-surfed. When I stopped in to retrieve my stored items a couple of weeks later, all the pieces fell together and it all made sense . . . the random marbles, the psychotic radio, the missing soap, the magic sugar bowl, the sweeping lights, and the far-flung blankets. It was a kid.

When I happened by the neighbors' that day, another ancient darling neighbor lady was over for tea, reminiscing. She, being quite privy to the neighborhood doings, sympathized with me and told me that when she was a girl, a little boy who lived in that shack had died of smallpox or some such and the parents built the new house right alongside it, abandoning the shack. She said they kept on building on the new house 'til their deaths. It was a lovely visit, with plenty of details and *a-has!* exchanged. I thanked the ladies and packed up. As I drove off to populate my new digs, I marveled at how hard that kid worked to get my attention! Oblivious, inebriated, passed out cold, or in a rush to get to work, I couldn't have been an easy one to haunt. But really I got to enjoy him as a roommate a few scant weeks of the six months I lived there, acknowledging him with a "Hi honey, I'm home," each time I came in the front door.

I often wonder if that priest knew his business . . .
I also wonder if the kid attached himself to me.

—ALIX BENEDICT

The house ghost is usually a harmless and well-meaning creature. It is put up with as long as possible. It brings good luck to those who live with it. I remember two children who slept with their mother and sisters and brothers in one small room. In the room was also a ghost. They sold herrings in the Dublin streets, and did not mind the ghost much, because they knew they would always sell their fish easily while they slept in the "ha'nted" room.

—W. B. YEATS, *CELTIC TWILIGHT*

Castle in the Air

What's eerier than the ghost of a child? What about the ghosts of hundreds of children? Preston Castle is an old boys' school in Ione, California. Built in 1890, it looms above the sleepy little gold rush town, peering down upon the vineyards and scraggly pines with half-shuttered window-eyes and a toothless brick grin. It was built to house the Preston School of Industry, a school whose intent was to reform and rehabilitate juvenile offenders. While it did just that, during the Great Depression (and other times in history) it also happened that families who could not afford to feed their children would leave their sons there. Sometimes they came back for the boys. Other times, they did not. The ages of children ranged from seven to seventeen. The grand plans for the school included seventy-seven rooms on five floors, though the top floors never saw completion and today remain in a ruinous state. It shuttered its doors in 1960 but somehow escaped demolition. It endured, crumbling, until 2001, when the Preston Castle Foundation took it over. It is officially now a California Historical Landmark and is listed on the National Register of Historic Places. It seems that the castle has been saved! The foundation works to raise funds for the restoration of the entire property.

One of the ways they make money is by offering tours. You can visit during the day most days of the week, but if you are at all inclined toward the paranormal, then an overnight ghost tour is for you!

You'll not be surprised to learn that I had the privilege of doing this overnight tour with my beloved mom and two of my spookiest sisters. When we arrived, the moon was on the rise, nearly full and streaming through the holes in the roof to the floorboards below. Bats swept in and out of the rafters just below the nest of white barn owls that screeched all evening long. It was as if we'd been transported to the California branch of Hogwarts and all manner of witchery was waiting us. The tour instructions advise that you—should you plan to sleep—bring your own sleeping bag. While you

might think you couldn't possibly stay up all night, as you once did in days of your youth, I'm here to tell you it is not the type of place where you'll settle down to rest. Sleep, in my humble opinion, is entirely out of the question. Picture the interior: endless corridors of peeling paint, faded wallpaper, and cracked windowpanes. Lathe wood exposed and abandoned beds in the infirmary (where, incidentally, my sister felt her hair pulled by some ghostly fingers). An empty pool in the basement where the boys were deloused after "check-in." Rusted showerheads peeking out from chipped tiles in the massive communal shower room. It is the setting for a horror novel and, at once, beautiful and terrifying. Unlike other abandoned properties, Preston Castle has just enough upkeep to give the appearance that someone still lives there.

It was in a small room in the basement that we met the ghost of William. Our docent for the evening had us sit in a circle as she gave us the basics for the night: we should stay together, and please not wander off into other rooms. We would, she assured us, have a chance to see all the floors of the castle, but because some of them were hazardous (the floor could cave in or worse), we should stay together. There was another group that night, so we shouldn't assume all noises would be paranormal. She encouraged us to take photos and record at random. And then she told us about William. Having been a docent there for many years, spending hours giving tours and waiting the time between alone in the house, she became accustomed to certain spirits that would make regular contact with her. One, she said, was that of a little boy, probably about ten years old. He visited her often, and one day she was walking about the property of the castle when she found three graves. One of them was clearly a child's grave and was marked with the name William. Assuming that this was her regular boyish ghoul, she began addressing him by name. Shortly after telling us her story, she began to call him.

"William . . . William . . ." she beckoned. "Won't you come to see us? Please come and play."

> **"Won't you come to see us? Please come and play."**

She went on like this for a bit of time. Someone had an EVP recorder and had set it in the middle of the room. The docent handed my mom a pair of witching rods and asked her to use them to see if she could find anything. All this time I was casually snapping photos. I took one of the doorway behind us, the windows, the floor, the witching rod experiment, and so on.

The night continued with a number of amazing rooms, eerie noises, and the aforementioned hair pulling. There seemed to be something electric in the air in what was once the library. The old swimming pool in the basement was disturbingly quiet. My other sister burst into tears in the shower room. All in all, it was a long, emotional night for many of us. As for me, I was in awe of every crumbling wall and hallway shadow.

It wasn't until a couple of days later, when I had made it home and uploaded all of my pictures from my digital camera, that I found quite a shock. The photo I first took when our tour guide was calling in William had an orb in it, but not just any orb. It was two-thirds of the way down the length of the doorway, around the height where one might expect to see the head of a child. And, upon closer inspection, it actually looked very much like the face of a child. Other notable photos included dozens and dozens of orbs in the library (to be fair, it was dusty there), which appeared in only one of the many photos I snapped in a row. Above the creepy pool a bright pink blob of light hovered, surely a trick of the light.

Is Preston Castle haunted? You can find out for yourself. Just visit their website (*prestoncastle.com*), where you can book a tour. They offer paranormal overnights, Halloween events, photography tours, and more. You can also make a donation to the Preston Castle Foundation to help save the castle.

The Thing That Moans in the Woods

"What is it? What the devil is it?" I asked.
   "That Damned Thing!" he replied, without turning his head. His voice was husky and unnatural. He trembled visibly.

—Ambrose Bierce, *That Damned Thing*

The siren song of legend: a keening, cooing melody that leads one toward the craggy shipwreck of death. The mermaid's ballad: luring you closer to the frigid hands of a riptide, as you stumble, enchanted, to a watery grave.

A Lamentable Encounter

Should you find yourself alone driving along an isolated road anywhere in Mexico, take heed—La Llorona, The Weeping Woman, wanders the country in search of her children. As legend has it, she is the ghost of a woman who drowned her own children and then herself in a river. Her cries, not unlike those of the Irish banshee, are like a woman in deepest mourning. She can appear alongside a road as a hitchhiker but has also been seen near lakes and rivers, reportedly looking for her children. She is beautiful, with long, dark hair and very long fingernails and dressed in either flowing gowns of white or black. It is said that after an encounter with her, the victim is left feeling completely drained and exhausted, which has led to her association with vampires. In some accounts, she is—like the banshee—a harbinger of grave illness and death and may exist as a warning.

The banshee's horrid scream: frightening you to attention, unable to stop the inevitable death or—at best—grave illness of someone dear to you. All of these noises, in their own entrancing way, are the sounds of death. They draw you nigh though you know not what you do.

There are many sounds associated with ghosts, at least by way of the ghost story. The creaking of floorboards, the tapping on the wall, a loud and unexpected slam of a door. The moaning, chain-rattling ghost of Marley in *A Christmas Carol* harkens back to the idea of a banshee appearing as a warning with its mournful howl. Ghosts emit sounds of torture or plaintive cries, a phantom song or a whisper.

These are not at all the kinds of sounds you are about to hear about in the following story, which also takes place in the foothills of California, although a bit farther north than Preston Castle. This is one of those stories that, when I first heard it (standing not 100 yards from the cabin in the story, mind you), inspired a vague wave of nausea. My pulse quickened, my throat felt dry. And so, naturally, I asked to hear it again. And again. At last, I cajoled my friend Chris into committing it to the page, and it is now here to terrify you. I will caution you, my faithful friends, if you are not reading this in the bright light of day, please pull your blankets tighter and be sure your candle will burn for hours to come, for you will not be able to sleep.

Christopher Ward has been a prehistoric and historic archeologist in California for more than twenty years, specializing in California prehistory, faunal analysis, and the California gold rush era. He serves as a field specialist, researcher, analyst, and author and has participated in numerous archeological and anthropological studies throughout California, Nevada, Mexico, and Guatemala. He is the author of *Cemeteries of the Western Sierra.* And this is his story:

The Incident at Indian Spring

It was just after dusk one summer evening at the property in rural Northern California when the incident took place. (The fact that this didn't happen in the middle of the night actually made it spookier somehow.) It was midsummer, and dark was just beginning

to settle, around 9:30 or 10 at night. There were a few clouds forming, but the breeze was hot as I worked on the small structure on my property—Casa Refugio. I'd been fixing up this little cabin so that my then-girlfriend (now wife) and I could start staying on the property more often, as we were beginning to work out future plans to build a house and a life together.

I was hanging out in Casa Refugio fixing things and trying to dial it in to make it a comfortable place to stay overnight and was finally starting to wind down for the evening. The cabin had double doors that were open, but I closed them and bolted them shut to keep mosquitoes and other critters at bay as I settled in. I was alone

on the property and had no pets or other companions at the time. I should also mention that the property adjoins my grandparents' land, and I have spent the majority of my childhood and better part of my life on that land. There were no pathways, no wooded areas, and few sounds or animals that I did not know by heart.

I was just starting to kick back when I heard it. A *loud*, long, and low moan. My immediate thought was that it was a sound traveling up from the valley below—there is a farm there that has miniature burros, and they've been known to make strange noises, especially to the unaccustomed ear. Within seconds, however, it was clear this was no donkey. A low note began again, resonating in a way that is almost indescribable. It was guttural, or the lowest of a baritone range, so low that the cabin and the ground, the items in the window-sill, all began to vibrate. There's a musical term—hemi-sync—when a sound is felt more than heard.

I began to feel very isolated—up on that moun-taintop, all alone. As I inched toward the door, the sound truncated. It was as if the sound were in a vacuum: there was no echo or lingering resonance; it just stopped. There was no further noise of crash-ing bushes, no rustling in the woods. I crept up to the door, and I—a grown man who's traveled the world, spelunking in underground caverns and sleeping overnight in legendary haunted boathouses—began to feel as frightened as a little child. All the while my mind was racing: if it couldn't be the *burritos*, then perhaps it was just a kid making sounds on a synthesizer that somehow carried up the hill? A joke to scare the neighbors? I opened the door, sure that I was about to come face-to-face with something horrific. I put one foot out the door, and saw: nothing. I began to ease outside, thinking surely I'd spot something unnamed or maybe some injured animal. Just as I started to get outside, it began again. Only this time, it was closer. Much closer.

> **I quickly stepped back into the room and could hear that it was getting closer still.**

Whereas before it was clearly down in the valley below (and eerie enough from there), now it was nearer. It was at once organic and electric, like a heartbeat but bellowing. It had this bass tone that again started everything around me vibrating with a low hum. I quickly stepped back into the room and could hear that it was getting closer still. Now, it seemed to be approaching fast, as if it were on a supersonic sprint up the mountain. Again it stopped. It completely died away. Only moments later, as I allowed a brief sense of ease, it started up again, this time probably not more than 100 feet away. I began to weigh my options: Should I stay where I was? Should I go out looking for it? It seemed to be coming toward me. The bellowing sound grew nearer still and things in my cabin went from vibrating to rattling, as if a small earthquake were taking place (or a tractor were raging past). The sound was growing stronger and stronger, now not more than fifty feet away, coming from the midst of a stand of black oaks just below the cabin.

And then it stopped. There was no lingering echo, no rustling leaves, crunching twigs, or branches breaking. Nothing. The sound simply ended.

Fast-forward a day later. By now, I had begun to think I had heard something that just couldn't be. My mind was playing tricks on me; it was a drone possibly, from the nearby airforce base; it was a freaking condor . . . I don't know. I just knew it was a sound I had never heard before and one that didn't make sense to me. It was completely biological: if it came from an animal, it was an animal I was not familiar with. Of course, supernatural beasts crossed my mind. I even thought, perhaps someone imported some kind of exotic animal I would never recognize. I had no explanation, but I tried to get my head around it in every way possible.

By the nature of my work—I am an archeologist—and my upbringing, I have spent hundreds of hours in the woods, in nature, in isolated places observing and recording the world around me. This was unlike anything I had ever heard.

In any case, a day after the incident, the neighbor's sixteen-year-old son came walking up to the property to say hello. With excitement I soon shared my story, fresh in my mind, with him. He listened, was interested and perhaps a little amused, but nothing more.

By the next evening, his story had changed big time. Shortly after I arrived on the property the next afternoon, the neighbor kid was quick after me. As I pulled up, he was right behind, and I could see he was wide-eyed. We chatted, and he started to tell me something that sent chills down my spine: just the night before (one night after what I'd experienced, and later

that same night I had shared the story with him), his father had heard a fantastically strange noise.

I headed down to visit with my neighbors and get his story: sure enough, he began describing something so like what I had experienced I could hardly believe it. He heard a low, moaning sound that reverberated. He heard crashing and thrashing about his property and even a loud plunge as something of great weight went into his pond. Like me, he has no livestock or animals. He did have a dog, who was tied up at the time and could not make that noise. He couldn't explain it, and he was just as stunned as I was to learn that I had heard the same noise the night prior.

To this day I have no explanation. I have not heard it since (thankfully), but I can never forget it, the Incident at Indian Spring.

—CHRIS A. WARD AS TOLD TO VARLA VENTURA

A Cautionary Tale

In Maidu stories, Kohuneje is a hairy, beastly monster, similar in description to Bigfoot and Dogmen. The Kohuneje lives in woodland areas and forests and eats human children.

What Big Eyes You Have:
Gigantic Ghosts of Welsh Lore

William Wirt Sikes, in his tome *British Goblins*, provides some frightening stories on the grotesque nature of ghosts, including a gigantic ghost spotted near the parish of Llantarnam, a suburb of Cwmbran in southeast Wales. As the story goes, a young man was coming home one night when he heard something approaching. It was so dark, at first he was unable to see anything, and so he pressed on. All of the sudden a tall figure stood before him, blocking his path: the ghost of a thin man who was so tall, the young man nearly fell over backward trying to see the top of it. Out of fear and with few options, the young man shouted, "What in the name of God are you? Out of my way, or I'll strike thee down!" The ghost disappeared slowly, and the young, terrified fellow could not venture on without taking a rest in the field, leaning against a cow for comfort.

There are many ghost stories which we do not feel at liberty to challenge.

—Sir Walter Scott, *Demonology and Witchcraft*

Chapter 2

Have Ghost, Will Travel

Haunted Places and the Ghosts That Love Them; Haunted Houses, Hotels, Hospitals, Cemeteries, and the Empire of the Dead

Where'er we tread 'tis haunted, holy ground.

—LORD BYRON, "CHILDE HAROLD'S PILGRIMAGE"

Home Is Where the Haunt Is

Fans of vintage horror fiction will no doubt nod their heads in agreement when I say that central to almost every ghost story is the haunted house. Generally, this house is an unoccupied flat or abandoned home, one of fine design with good bones. One that seems to be a real steal or a hidden treasure, at least before it was forsaken. But there is always a reason it sits empty.

One does not always identify the house as haunted at first. The protagonist, often the skeptic, refuses to believe in ghosts and accepts the dare of a friend or takes on the house at the prospect of low or free rent. Even as a person who has had paranormal encounters, I lived in one apartment that I refused to think was haunted. When I was moving in, I had a fairly intuitive friend who, upon putting the box down in the tiny bedroom, declared to me very matter-of-factly: "you won't be alone here long." Thinking she was making reference to my as-yet-to-be-identified live-in lover, I laughed it off. But she repeated again, very seriously this time, "I'm not kidding. There's someone else here."

A young woman living alone in a big city can find plenty to fear: the creepy guy outside at the bus stop, the group of men who step out of the shadows a block away. So the idea of an unseen force in my house didn't really bother me. Does the apartment door lock? That's usually enough.

> **"I'm not kidding. There's someone else here."**

It was about a month after moving in that I learned that there was, in fact, someone or *something* in the place. As so often happens with paranormal encounters, I had laid down my weary head close to midnight. I had drifted off to sleep, when I woke up to the feeling that something was sitting on the bed. It felt exactly like a cat climbing on the bed and pressing the covers down near your feet, and this is what I thought it was in my sleepy state. Until the split second later when I remembered that I did not have a cat. I sat up, my heart racing, and looked around the room. There was nothing to be seen—no glowing face or eyes at the foot of the bed, no shadowy figures in the room, which had light flooding in from the streetlamp below. I shook it off and was so tired that it didn't take long before I fell back asleep. No sooner had I fallen asleep than I was awoken *again* by the feeling of something sitting on the bed, though this time it was pressing down on my legs, rather than just next to my feet. This time I sat upright and put the light on. Eventually I fell back asleep . . . and it happened again, this time with the gentle pressure closer to my chest. After that, I decided to get up and do something else. It was just a two-room place, so I went to the other room, switching on all the lights, and busied myself unpacking a few remaining items and cleaning the kitchen until the light of day.

Whatever it was never returned (at least not in that form), but it certainly made its presence known to me.

In Edward Bulwer-Lytton's *The House and the Brain* (Lytton is best known for the infamous opening line, "It was a dark and stormy night"), a house is full of ghosts trapped in limbo by a hidden occult master's evil spell. In Richard Le Gallienne's story *The Haunted Orchard*, the sweet little country home that our hero lets for the summer gives way to an enchanted semblance of a once-living bride. Charles Mackay, an early nineteenth-century, Scottish-born poet, author, and songwriter, describes the haunted house in his infamous work *Extraordinary Popular Delusions and the Madness of Crowds*:

> Who has not either seen or heard of some house, shut up and uninhabitable, fallen into decay, and looking dusty and dreary, from which, at midnight, strange sounds have been heard to issue—aerial knockings—the rattling of chains, and the groaning of perturbed spirits?—a house that people have thought it unsafe to pass after dark, and which has

remained for years without a tenant, and which no tenant would occupy, even were he paid to do so? There are hundreds of such houses in England at the present day; hundreds in France, Germany, and almost every country of Europe, which are marked with the mark of fear—places for the timid to avoid, and the pious to bless themselves at, and ask protection from, as they pass—the abodes of ghosts and evil spirits.

Mackay does not, in fact, believe in ghosts and hauntings and later goes on to say that "in general, houses that have acquired this character have been more indebted for it to the roguery of living men than to accidents like these," by which he means the accidents of accidental ghosts.

And what of that abandoned house, down yonder lane, whose door is woven shut with the tendrils of ivy? Can a house be haunted not by a supernatural ghost, but by the memories of more glorious times, of times when the fire was warm on the hearth and the sound of children laughing was common within its walls? Can the madness of men, of our own guilt, of our desire to be like others and see what others see—as

Mackay believes—lead us to "see" ghosts? In this chapter we will travel from cemetery gate to underground Paris and learn, among other things, what becomes of a skeptic when they finally see a ghost.

Roll Up for the Mystery Tour

Sarah Winchester, heir to the Winchester rifle empire, left behind her legacy in a bizarre house in San Jose known as the Winchester Mystery House. Speculation has grown over the years as to what caused this reclusive woman to transform an eight-room farmhouse into a six-acre sprawling estate with odd angles, doors that go nowhere, a séance room, and stairs that lead into walls.

Her obsession with the continual building is said to have been to appease the spirits of those souls who died at the wrong end of a Winchester rifle, but a visit to the house reveals some pretty OCD tendencies. Stricken with grief at the loss of her baby at just six weeks old, followed by the death of her beloved husband fifteen years later, she relocated from Boston to the Santa Clara Valley with—quite literally—more money than she could ever spend. At one point her revenues from the Winchester Repeating Arms Company paid out at $1,000 a day, on top of the millions of dollars she received in cash. And this was in 1897—*without income tax.* Wander the thumping, bumping halls of this mansion, and you'll discover treasures such as these:

- The $25,000 storeroom, aka beautiful hoarding room, which holds unused stained glass, doors, doorknobs, tiles, rolls of wallpaper, and other architectural details that were never used. Winchester used to order extravagant pieces in bulk and decide later where to put them.

- Spiderwebs, which is one of her repeating themes throughout the house. Windows, in particular, feature this motif. The thirteenth bathroom contained thirteen of them. (Original Goth!)

She had all that wealth and nowhere to go. Sarah was a recluse, who often wore a veil in public and had a large hedge installed around the house to dissuade lookie-loos. She also had a lot of people after her money and was understandably cautious. She did, however, have a soft spot for children and would allow the neighbor girls in frequently to visit and play the organ in the ballroom. During the great 1906 earthquake (which left San Francisco in flaming ruins) Sarah was trapped in what is called her "daisy room" for a number of hours. Fearing it was a sign from the beyond (and keep in mind there was limited communication and no instant news of what had happened), she had construction halted on an entire wing of the house, leaving much of it today as it was then, with cracked plaster and peeling wallpaper.

Sarah was quirky if not socially awkward. In fact, President Theodore Roosevelt "stopped by" to say hello to the grande dame, but the servants were under strict orders to never let anyone pass through the ornate double doors of the main entrance. Sarah had had them sealed after the 1906 quake, and prior to that only three people had gained entry that way: Sarah and the two carpenters who installed them. When Teddy was asked to use the side or "servants" entrance, he promptly left.

When Sarah died in 1922, this wealthy heiress's safe was opened with much anticipation. However, instead of gold bricks and sparkling jewels, the contents were newspaper clippings including her infant daughter's obituary, a lock of her baby's hair, fishing lines, socks, and underwear.

A few years back I was offered a private, detailed tour of the grounds and mansion for myself and a few close friends and family. During the tour one of the younger children in the party needed to use the restroom, which was actually a floor below. Our tour guide frowned, as it is very easy to get lost in the many rooms and endless hallways, so he suggested we wait in a particular room until the child and accompanying adult could meet back up with us. We did, lingering and snapping a few photos, not moving much and chatting with the tour guide about his background and how he came to work at the mansion. Several minutes went by, and eventually our missing members rejoined the group. We continued wandering the corridors, balancing on the balconies and watching the sunset from one of Sarah's many spiderweb windows. After the tour was over, the person who had brought his child down to the bathroom told me that once they found the restroom, he waited just outside the door while the child went in. As he was waiting, he heard footsteps approaching and assumed someone was about to walk by. But he didn't see anyone. He said he could hear the footsteps and creakings from the floor above, but that the sound he'd heard was distinctly coming from the very hall he was standing in. He didn't mention it

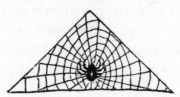

or remark on it right away because he didn't want to frighten the child. But he swears to this day he heard steps approaching and they were so loud he was sure he'd see another tour guide or person from our group walking up. The Winchester Mystery House does tours daily including special Friday the 13th Flashlight Tours. In early 2018, *Winchester*—the much-anticipated film about Sarah Winchester—was released.

If the Spirit Moves You

Dave Cruz is an Oakland, California, native who grew up surrounded by lore and urban legends: stories of witches, vampires, and even possessed dolls were often told at family gatherings. Strange things seemed to follow him around. Now the host of *Beyond the Strange* radio show (*beyondthe strange.com*), Dave revisits his favorite topics including ghosts, paranormal and unexplained encounters, and UFOs. He has been involved in two UFO sightings, one of which was a mass sighting by family and neighbors. He has graciously shared the story of his first-ever investigation, at the Lawler House.

The House with the Movable Ghosts

This is the story about my first real paranormal investigation. It started with a visit to Suisun City, California—not far from where I live. Suisun City, and especially the marina area of town, is a bit of a hotbed for paranormal activity. The city has a rich history, and the marina area was once home to many brothels and, consequently, many untimely deaths.

The Lawler House sits in the marina area, but it is not original to that section of town. It was actually built in the 1800s and moved to its present location in 1979.

I had been meaning to pay this historic home a visit, having heard a rumor that it might be haunted. My wife and I went to the museum, and there a docent gave us a basic tour, but she mostly talked about the construction and movement of the house. She didn't give us any info on who had built it or owned it or lived in it.

I asked if I could go upstairs (it's a three-story Victorian). She said I could, and my wife chose to stay down in the main lobby of the museum. Just as I got to the top of the stairs on the second floor, I began to feel very sick. It was hard to breathe, my chest felt heavy, and I actually thought I was having a heart attack. The thought actually went through my mind, perhaps I had pushed myself too hard on the stairs? I moved away from the spot where I was standing and instantly felt better. I moved back toward the same area I had been in and started feeling sick again. I did this a few more times until I finally decided to head down the stairs. I told my wife what had happened, and I asked the docent if she'd ever had anything strange happen upstairs. Her very matter-of-fact response was, "Oh, I don't go upstairs."

Her very matter-of-fact response was, "Oh, I don't go upstairs."

Not long after, I contacted a medium friend of mine who lived in the nearby foothills and asked her if she'd accompany me on another exploration of the house. We arranged an investigation.

Upon our arrival to the Lawler House, the medium went straight to the second floor. I went across the street to get something to drink and came back to start to climb the stairs, where I could see her sitting on the floor (of the second floor), writing in her notebook. I climbed the stairs to a spot where I began to feel sick again. Right then my friend said, "Stop. Stay where you are." (Which I of course did!)

"Walk toward me. Now go up toward the third floor—go to the middle of the stairs," she instructed.

Again, I did exactly as she requested. She then told me to stop—which I did.

"You are right in the middle of them."

I started feeling very emotional at this point, a very strong feeling but different from the sickness and pain I'd experienced before. My friend coached me to remain calm, telling me to think of a white light, ground myself, and try to relax. I did exactly as she said, and I started to feel better. As the sadness and ill feelings faded, she began to read me what she had written. It was the description of an established gentleman, a man in his mid-forties, who had lived in the house and died in the house.

> "You are right in the middle of them."

It was later that I did research and discovered that the Mr. Lawler, after whom the house is named, did in fact die in the house. He passed away from a heart attack.

I have EVP recordings from sessions we've done there. I'm not sure if it was his residual energy I picked up on or if it was his ghost. I do know that I will never forget that feeling.

—DAVE CRUZ AS TOLD TO VARLA VENTURA

All the Pretty Little Horses

The Pony Express was in existence between April 1860 and October 1861. This rapid mail service operated between St. Joseph, Missouri, and Sacramento, California. One of the old Pony Express stations is still standing in Hollenberg Station in Kansas. Hollenberg's administrator, Duane Durst, has many times heard the sounds of footsteps on the second floor and of furniture being moved, although he knows that the upper floor is completely empty. But he and others have also heard the sounds of horses whinnying and stamping. Late at night there has been heard the creaking of saddles and the pounding of hooves, as of ponies galloping past. "When the wind blows," says Durst, "you hear a lot of creaking and groaning, and the sounds of someone upstairs."

— RAYMOND BUCKLAND, *THE WEISER FIELD GUIDE TO GHOSTS*

Stay with Me: Haunted Hotels of America

Second only to the haunted house for setting is the haunted hotel. The following hotels are not only haunted but, at the time of writing, are actually still in operation or about to make a grand reopening, meaning you can potentially go and see for yourself what sort of spirit may be lurking. In nearly every town in the United States, if not the world, you're likely to find a hotel or inn that claims to be haunted. I've included here just a few of my favorites. If you're like me and enjoy a good scream in the middle of the night, put these spots on your bloody bucket list right away.

The Stanley Hotel in Estes Park, Colorado

The inspiration for Stephen King's Overlook Hotel in his novel *The Shining*, the Stanley Hotel, is home to more than one ghost. Although the infamous movie starring

Jack Nicholson was not filmed here, rooms 407, 217, 401, and 418 are all reported to be haunted by a variety of spirits. And if the Stanley is all booked, try staying in the nearby Baldplate Inn, a historic, 100-year-old inn with its own resident ghost. Ethel Mace, the original owner of the place, was reportedly a staunch prohibitionist in her lifetime and has been known to occasionally send cocktails flying off the table.

> *I never worry about being driven to drink; I just worry about being driven home.*
>
> —W. C. FIELDS

The Baker Hotel in Mineral Wells, Texas

One of the most famous historic hotels in Texas, the Baker Hotel opened its lobby doors in 1929, as a fourteen-floor luxury hotel with modern amenities perfect for its legendary guests. Past celebs that made a stay over include Judy Garland, Marlene Dietrich, Clark Gable, Pat Boone, and Lyndon Johnson, and it's rumored even Bonnie and Clyde checked in. It boasted the first Olympic-size hotel swimming pool—filled with the area's therapeutic mineral waters—as well as air-conditioning and automatic light controls.

While the hotel prospered for over twenty years and was considered a grand destination, known for its restorative spa, by the 1950s its popularity—and the population of the area post-WWII—began to decline. Owner Earl Baker shuttered the doors to the public in 1963, though the hotel had a brief revival in 1965 when it was leased from the Baker family. But in 1967, Earl Baker died in the hotel's sprawling Baker Suite. The group who had leased and tried to revive the hotel eventually gave up and closed it in 1972. And so it has remained, not unlike the set of *American Horror Story: Hotel*, for years.

According to hotel guests during its heyday, ghosts were present even then. There are rumors that a bloody, naked woman can be seen on the seventh floor, supposedly the jilted mistress of the hotel manager, who took her own life by leaping from the balcony. Another young woman died trying to leap to the pool from her balcony. Others have claimed to see the ghost of a man who was killed by an elevator door. Since the hotel doors have been closed, paranormal investigators have conducted numerous investigations. Renovations began in 2014, and the restoration crew reports doors slamming, the sounds of plates and clattering from the dining room, and the vision of a woman in white passing through the hall. During a 2012 episode of *Ghost Adventures*, many voices were caught on tape, including the recording of a little girl saying "momma." There's also an eerie bit of footage of a door opening slowly within the mistress's room. Ghost hunters should take heart: the hotel

is currently well on track for a grand restoration that will convert the once 450 rooms into 157 luxury suites, revive the famous spa, and allow for 11,000 square feet of retail space. At the time of this writing, no official grand-opening date had been announced, but keep an eye out at *thebakerhotel.com* for your chance to experience all of the glam and ghosts in the future digs.

The St. Anthony Hotel
in San Antonio, Texas

The "jewel of downtown San Antonio," the St. Anthony Hotel, debuted its Italian marble interiors to the public in 1909, making it officially the first luxury hotel in San Antonio. A host to the presidents and celebrities alike, the hotel has seen everyone from Eleanor Roosevelt to George Clooney walk through its doors. It's also home to many ghosts, spotted over the years.

Some of the most notorious include the Lady in Red, who is seen wandering the corridors and appearing in the women's restroom while guests were washing their hands or just leaving. They report seeing a woman dressed all in red enter a stall and then just disappear. One of the rooms (536) is said to be the site of a suicide when a man who had committed a gruesome murder at the nearby Gunther Hotel checked himself into the St. Anthony. When confronted by the police, he shot himself in the head.

On more than one occasion, guests have checked into the hotel and gone to their rooms to discover that they are already occupied—usually by a couple enjoying cocktails. When the guests complain to management, the hotel promptly sends up security to figure out why someone was in the wrong room and they always find the room empty.

The St. Anthony underwent a full-scale renovation between 2013 and 2015, but prior to this I happened to visit the St. Anthony myself. I checked in with my sister, staying just one night before heading farther south to visit an elderly relative. I had two experiences there. The first was on the tenth floor. I later read up on the hotel and learned that tenth-floor sightings were fairly common, though I did not know the history nor haunted history at the time. We'd taken the elevator up to head out onto the terrace just before sunset. As we entered

the terrace and I was closing the glass door behind us, I looked back down the long hallway toward the elevators. There, for just a brief moment, I saw the dark shadow of something—about the height of a woman of medium build—sort of swish across the narrow hallway as if she'd come right out of a room and walked right toward the elevators. I had the impression she was in a dress of some kind, something more formal. As soon as I saw it, my brow furrowed, and my sister saw the look on my face. She asked what was wrong, and I said, "I saw something. I'm just going to go look and see if it's a person." So I quickly walked back down the hall to check if I had just seen the shadow of someone going for the elevator. No one was there. It didn't seem like enough time for someone to have gotten in the elevator, but I suppose it was possible. I shrugged it off and headed back out.

After an evening of exploring the River Walk area in San Antonio (and getting tattoos!), we finally went to bed. My sister sleeps with earbuds in, so she did not hear anything in the night. But all night long I kept hearing clicks and clacks and smacking sounds coming from the little bathroom. At one point, I was sure I heard the sound of something hitting the floor—as if one of our toiletries had smacked against the tile. I got

Isn't That Crazy?

After finding out about the shocking elements like stabbing, "nudity," and a flushing toilet, Alfred Hitchcock was unable to convince the movie moguls at Paramount Pictures that *Psycho* was worth the investment. So Hitchcock used another tactic: he offered to take no salary himself (he normally earned a sizable sum) as director of the picture. They went for it.

up, fully expecting to find something on the floor when I went into the bathroom, but there was nothing there. I admit I slept fitfully, but had no other experiences to speak of. Naturally, I can't wait to go back.

The Hotel Monteleone
in New Orleans, Louisiana

Anyone who is up for a good ghost adventure knows that New Orleans is a hot spot—and staying in a haunted luxury hotel in the French Quarter pretty much takes the cake. With its proximity to witchy digs and bars and high-thread-count sheets, the Hotel Monteleone will check all your boxes. Oh, and did I mention it has a revolving bar?

Established in 1886, the hotel boasts a rich literary history: Ernest Hemmingway, Tennessee Williams, Anne Rice, and Stephen Ambrose have all graced its halls. But perhaps more famous are the hotel's ghostly guests. According to the hotel's own website, there's a restaurant door that opens and closes almost every night in spite of being locked; a haunted elevator that stops on the wrong floor, where patrons spot ghostly children at play; the spirits of former employees; the apparition of William "Red" Wildemere—who died in the hotel of natural causes; and a friendly tot named Maurice Begere, who died in the hotel and is frequently seen near the room where he passed.

The Silver Queen Hotel
in Virginia City, Nevada

First built in 1876, the Silver Queen is a quirky hotel with frequent guest reports of haunted activity. One couple heard the sound of a banjo being played loudly in the next room, but discovered the room empty upon investigation. Another guest heard someone arguing loudly in the hallway, but when they opened the door to confront the fighting couple, no one was there. Many guests have reported knocks (and even sometimes pounding) on their hotel room doors but discover nobody on the other side. Room 15 is said to be one of the most haunted.

The Silver Queen's location can't be beat: the heart of historic Virginia City, where ghosts of past sins permeate the air. This hotel is also the starting point of the town's ghost tour, and I have it on good authority that they make a mean Bloody Mary. Nearby, the Gold Hill Hotel and Saloon has a few ghosts of its own. The oldest existing hotel in Nevada, it opened in 1859 amid the booming gold and silver mining heyday. The hotel's most notorious ghost is Rosie, so named for the distinct smell of roses that many guests over the years have detected upon entering room 4. She is playful and moves objects and personal belongings around the room and often turns off the lights. There's also William, another mischievous but harmless ghost who is thought to be the spirit of one of the miners who died in a horrible fire at the nearby Yellowjacket Mine. He is often detected by the smell of pipe tobacco. There are also reports of the sound of children laughing accompanied by the smell of baking cookies.

> **There are also reports of the sound of children laughing accompanied by the smell of baking cookies.**

The Dorrington Hotel
in Dorrington, California

Poor Rebecca Dorrington. Though the town is named for her, she died in a fatal fall down a flight of stairs at this hotel back in 1870. Today's guests report banging doors, flashing lights, and even moving furniture. Some have even claimed to witness a phantom-reenactment of the terrible tumble down the stairs.

The Green Mountain Inn
in Stowe, Vermont

From the outside, you would never guess that this charming 105-guest-room inn is haunted. But according to *hauntedrooms.com*, some claim a spirit from the 1800s has haunted the hotel since it was opened. And that spirit has more than a semblance of personality: old Boots Berry is the inn's former horseman and was so named because of his love of tap dance. Boots was born in the hotel servants' quarters and beloved by the townspeople for his heroic rescue of a stagecoach. But Boots also loved to drink and was eventually fired because of it. Boots became a drifter, though he made his way back to the town of Stowe. In 1902 Boots saved a child from a rooftop during a major snowstorm but slipped and fell during the rescue. He died, but guests say they can hear the sound of boots tapping on the roof.

The Holbrooke Hotel
in Grass Valley, California

This gold rush hotel once saw its share of famous folk from literary celebs like Mark Twain and Bret Harte to presidential dignitaries Ulysses S. Grant and Grover Cleveland. It was also host to ruffians, gamblers, and even that illicit highwayman Black Bart. Today some of its most famous visitors are from the Great Beyond. Considered one of the most haunted hotels in the California foothills, sightings at this hotel include the ghost of Black Bart, a Victorian-era maid, a woman in a floral dress spotted in the kitchen, ghostly children playing in the hall, men counting money in the dining hall, and a beautiful blonde woman ascending and descending the stairway. Guests of the hotel and frequenters of the bar claim to hear the sounds of chains dragging along with countless rattles, tapping, and knocking on doors.

> **Guests of the hotel and frequenters of the bar claim to hear the sounds of chains dragging along with countless rattles, tapping, and knocking on doors.**

The Beverly Hills Hotel and Bungalows
in Beverly Hills, California

The epitome of old-school Hollywood, you'll find the Beverly Hills Hotel on—where else?—Sunset Boulevard in Beverly Hills. The hotel, which was first established in 1912 (before Beverly Hills even existed), has changed owners a number of times, but in spite of its age the glam has not worn off. During its heyday (1930s–1950s) Humphrey Bogart, Grace Kelly, Marilyn Monroe, Elizabeth Taylor, Marlene Dietrich, Rudolph Valentino, Mary Pickford, and Will Rogers were all guests. More recently, celebrities like Leonardo DiCaprio and Tom Cruise mingle among the guests.

Countless famous movies have been filmed here. But there is one type of guest who seems to linger long after checkout time: the ghostly kind. While numerous sightings have occurred over the years, the most famous are the ghosts of Harpo Marx and the composer Rachmaninoff, both of whom are seen in or near the bungalows. (Interestingly, the ghost of Harpo Marx is sometimes spotted in New York City's Algonquin Hotel along with the ghost of Dorothy Parker!) Nearby, Chateau Marmont is said to still be haunted by the spirit of John Belushi, who died of a drug overdose in Bungalow 3 in 1982. And the ghost of Marilyn Monroe lingers in the lobby of The Hollywood Roosevelt on Hollywood Boulevard. Her reflection has been spotted on more than one occasion, checking her hair and lipstick, in the mirror that hangs there (which was once in a suite Monroe frequently stayed in). The ghost of actor Montgomery Clift has also been spotted outside his favorite room at the Roosevelt—room 928.

Gadabout Town

The Hollywood Forever Cemetery in Hollywood, California, is the final resting place of many celebrities, including heartthrob of the silver screen Rudolph Valentino. During the summer movies are shown at this theater, projected on the side of his crypt. It is said that the ghost of his dog—a Great Dane named Kabar—haunts his grave. As for Valentino's ghost, it has been reported in his former bedroom and among the halls of his mansion in Beverly Hills, on the porch of his beach house in Oxnard, in the costume department of Paramount Pictures, at an apartment complex in Hollywood, and at the Santa Maria Inn in Santa Maria.

The Queen Anne Hotel
in San Francisco, California

First built as a boarding school known as The Mary Lake School for Girls by Senator James G. Fair, the Queen Anne Hotel opened its doors to young ladies in 1890. But by 1896 it was closed due to financial difficulties. Though it survived the 1906 earthquake (and subsequent fires), it remained closed until 1980, when it finally reopened as an upscale bed-and-breakfast after undergoing an extensive restoration. It is a hotbed of paranormal activity thanks to the frequently sighted specter of former headmistress of the finishing school, Mary Lake. She is said to haunt room 410, which was once her office, but has also been seen or felt throughout the hotel. Guests report the sensation of being tucked in in the middle of the night, unexplainable cold spots, and moved objects in their rooms. (How sweet!)

Standard Procedure: Haunted Hospitals and Institutions

It's a mad world, my masters.

—HERMAN CHARLES MERIVALE

When you're running screaming from the lobby of the Horror Hotel, you'll soon find yourself on the outskirts of town. In your blind fear of what might be behind you, you'll not notice that you've run straight through the rusting gate of the unkempt grounds of an abandoned hospital. By the time you realize where you are, it will be too late. While the haunted house can be visited upon a dare and the guest of the hotel may not know it is haunted when they check in, the haunted institution takes another degree of fortitude. Perhaps it is the grave-robbing foundation of medical knowledge that lends an eerie feeling to hospital corridors or the juxtaposition of a place once so clean and sanitary now anything but. Maybe it's the echoes of madhouse patients, still lost to the shock therapy of their "curing" years or the simple fact that people do die in hospitals. Or maybe it's just that hospitals, new or old, abandoned or occupied, are a place that most of us not in the medical profession would just as soon avoid. The following is just a smattering of the now-defunct asylums and institutions reputed to be haunted.

Nursing a Grudge

Able to house fifty patients, Waverly Hills opened in 1910 to accommodate tuberculosis patients. Over the years, additional structures were built to house more patients, including the 1914 construction of a children's ward, which housed both sick children and children whose parents were hospitalized there. By 1961 the use of the antibiotic streptomycin to treat tuberculosis rendered the hospital unnecessary. It closed down but reopened the following year as a home for the geriatric, though other patients with mental or physical disabilities were housed there as well. By 1982 the facility had been shut down again on allegations of abuse. Not surprisingly, rumors of patient mistreatment over the years include human experimentation, abuse, violence, and neglect. After a failed attempt to convert it into a prison, the shuttered estate was purchased by a couple that has embraced its ghoulish past. As they work on restoration, they host ghost hunts, photography tours, a Halloween haunted house, and even a laser light show. All proceeds go toward the restoration. Be on the lookout for phantom nurses, painful howls, and all manner of things that go bump in the night.

The House Up on the Hill

Few former institutions have a reputation like that of Hill View Manor in Newcastle, Pennsylvania. Built and opened in 1926 as the Lawrence County Home for the Aged, it also served as a poor farm and housed not only the elderly but also the severely impoverished and the mentally ill. The first residents were the facility directors, Perry D. Snyder and his wife Mary A. Snyder, their two children, twelve staff members, and twenty inmates. Mr. and Mrs. Snyder remained until 1944, when they were removed from their post and accused of incompetence. (They were in their late seventies.)

The home continued to operate under a new director, and the Snyders were actually allowed to stay on for a number of years. However, the Snyders, with Mrs. Snyder ill, were essentially evicted. It is believed their daughter also died around this time. In 1977 the home was "rebranded" as Hill View Manor. Hill View closed in 2004. The building and its grounds, which include a 100-grave cemetery, went up for sale and are now owned by a private company.

Hill View is thought by many to be one of the most haunted places in the United States. Residents who died (many by suicide) are thought to still rattle around the place. Over the years countless investigations have turned up volumes of evidence, including video, EVP recordings, and photos. Hill View offers history tours and allows both public and private investigations for a fee. In 2017 they were host to both a psychic fair and a paranormal conference, and more events are planned in the future.

Hell House for Rent

Northampton State Hospital in Northampton, Massachusetts, was home to thousands of mentally ill people throughout the course of its 200-year history. According to the website *northamptonstatehospital.org*, established to preserve the history of the hospital, it was "built to cure the insane in the Moralist tradition—a branch of Heroic medicine which focused on placing the ill in beautiful environ to stabilize the mind." In spite of its intentions, it was dubbed "Hell" by patients and their families and was eventually shut down in the mid-1990s. Visitors to the site claimed to hear the squeak of a ghostly wheelchair coming down the hall, doors slamming at random, and disembodied footsteps. In the 2000s most of the hospital's buildings were demolished, and a new apartment was built in its place.

Feeling Feeble

Originally known as Eastern Pennsylvania State Institution for the Feeble-Minded and Epileptic, this state hospital for the mentally and physically disabled opened to patients in 1908. It quickly became overcrowded, and over the years many expansions were made. With thousands of patients, the Pennhurst State School and Hospital could not meet demands financially or physically. In the 1960s and 1970s, allegations of abuse began to surface at Pennhurst. A court document from the federal district court case, Halderman v. Pennhurst State School and Hospital, specifies many horrific incidents, including excessive use of restraints—both chemical and physical—along with beatings, unusually long periods of solitary confinement, and filthy conditions for both the patients and the staff. The Halderman family, whose son, Teri Halderman, was an abused patient for more than ten years, initiated a lawsuit that eventually led to the exposure of the dreadful conditions and subsequent closing of the hospital. Ghost hunts over the years have reported slamming doors, footsteps, and unexplained tapping, knocking, and scratching sounds. The ghost of a little girl has been seen wandering the halls. According to the website *preservepennhurst.org*, as of 2015, the Pennhurst Memorial and Preservation Alliance entered into an agreement with the Department of Military and Veterans Affairs along with the Pennsylvania State Historic Preservation Office for the purchase of the superinten-

> **The ghost of a little girl has been seen wandering the halls.**

dents' residence with the long-range goal of making it an interpretive center and museum for disabilities.

Losing Your Patients

Originally built for the hundreds of employees of the Santa Fe Railroad, the Linda Vista Community Hospital in Los Angeles, California, opened in 1904. The railroad industry was booming—so much so that Linda Vista was just one of four hospitals constructed by the company. It remained in operation until the late 1970s and was ultimately sold in 1980 to another health care company. Under new management, the 150-bed infirmary saw a spike in death rates, some from gunshot wounds and stabbings. Claims over the years included gross neglect and mistreatment of patients and even "disappeared" patients who were said to become part of human experiments. The hospital was both a treating and surgical facility

> **Claims over the years included gross neglect and mistreatment of patients and even "disappeared" patients who were said to become part of human experiments.**

as well as a mental institution. It closed its ER services in 1989 and by 1991 closed altogether. The setting for many movies, TV shows, and rock videos (Nine Inch Nails filmed "Closer" here), the Linda Vista Community Hospital has served as a decaying, haunted backdrop ever since.

The ghostly legends that haunt its halls include the wandering souls of patients who died there (or, more frighteningly were "disappeared" and used in experiments) as well as the ghost of a doctor who was supposedly killed on the grounds by angry gang members who blamed him for the death of one of their own. Paranormal investigations over the years include *Ghost Adventures'* overnight investigation, complete with an exploration of the incinerator room and human ashes. Over the years EVP recordings have picked up sounds from humming to faint screams, and one ghost hunter claims he was scratched extensively on his back and many more report the feeling of heaviness or "dark" energy upon entering.

On a more cheery note, the hospital was renovated and turned into senior housing in 2015.

The Minnesota State Fair Grounds are haunted by a rather unusual ghost: that of a prized pig!

Fright Farm

The Ramsey County Poor Farm in Maplewood, Minnesota, was established in 1918 to house and help the indigent of society. The barn, which still stands and is now part of the Ramsey County fairgrounds, once housed more than 100 cows that provided milk for the residents here and at other county institutions. Beside the farm is a rolling patch of land which, to the untrained

eye, looks like an undeveloped plot but is actually what remains of the Poor Farm Cemetery, established in 1893. According to Ramsey County's website:

> A road was graded so the horse-drawn hearse could get though the hilly pasture. The graves were dug by hand and were marked with wooden stakes. There were no burials during the winter because of frozen ground. Instead, the deceased were stored in a cave-like place at the farm and Mother Nature froze them. The cave was near the pigpen to mask the smell when the spring thaw came. The names of the buried were kept in a ledger which was later transcribed and published through a joint effort of the Maplewood Area Historical Society and Park Genealogical Books. There were many John and Jane Does.

The Poor Farm Cemetery serves as the final resting place for 3,000 people who could not afford burial

elsewhere—about a third of these are unknown or unclaimed bodies. Although part of the cemetery is now under White Bear Avenue and other structures have been built on parts of it, the remaining cemetery has been preserved as a historic park. You can still visit the unmarked graves, where paranormal activity has been reported over the years. Both in the day and at night, visitors have reported figures in the cemetery that would quickly disappear, the sound of approaching footsteps, and the wail of a baby. Each year in October the Ramsey County Sheriff's Office transforms the old farm building into Fright Farm, one of the best haunted houses in the state.

A Gruesome Past

Along the picturesque shore of White Bear Lake in Minnesota there is a plaque preserving a story that—if it weren't for this little bit of history set in brass—would be altogether forgotten. The pedestrian path winds directly past the site of once-sacred burial mounds and a rather gruesome event.

It happened that in this area, along the shores of this lake, the ancestral Dakota had nine burial mounds, dated from 1400 to 1700 CE. As settlers moved into the territory in the 1800s and the affluent built vacation homes beside the lake, the mounds became a tourist attraction. One was even the foundation for a makeshift summer gazebo, within which landowner William F. Markowe placed a little table and chairs. The gazebo was blown away during a storm, and in 1889 an accident occurred that resulted in the demolishing of the burial mound.

A horse-drawn carriage full of passengers was passing through from Stillwater when the horses were spooked. The coach flipped over, and many of the passengers were injured. One, Charles Wheeler, was killed. His sister, Nellie, was hurt and sued the village of White Bear Lake. Although she did not win the lawsuit, the town ordered the mound flattened and the road straightened out.

Grave goods were removed from the mound along with nineteen skeletons, which were all loaded up onto a train car and sent south to the Minnesota Historical Society in St. Paul. However, the museum would only accept the artifacts and refused the human remains. And so the nineteen skeletons were loaded back into a

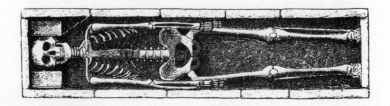

boxcar and sent north. Seventeen of the skeletons were buried at the nearby Union Cemetery. The other two skeletons were buried "near the property" where the burial mound once stood.

While residents of the area make no claims to ghosts, in nearby Matoska Park there have been sightings of a woman wandering near the gazebo and frequent unexplained screeches and screams.

Thirteen To-Die-For Haunted Cemeteries

1. The Archer Woods Cemetery in Justice, Illinois—a suburb of Chicago—is haunted by a weeping woman in white, who is sometimes heard sobbing. Other specters include a black coach-hearse pulled by a team of insane horses and carrying the glowing coffin of a child.

2. The Myrtle Hill Cemetery in Valley City, Ohio, is known to be haunted by a witch. Find her grave marked with a heavy sphere.

3. The Rose Hill Cemetery in Matawan, New Jersey, has generations of accounts of strange noises, eerie lights, and ghosts galore.

4. De Smet, South Dakota, is most famous for being the little town in Laura Ingalls Wilder's classic novel *Little Town on the Prairie*. It is here that the Ingalls family homestead still stands and is said to be haunted to this day. Many members of the Ingalls family are buried in the De Smet Cemetery, including Charles, Caroline, Mary, Carrie, Grace, and the infant son of Laura and Almanzo. (Laura, Almanzo, and her daughter are buried in Mansfield, Missouri.) Eerie lights and other strange sounds and unexplained specters have long been reported at the De Smet Cemetery.

5. Should you visit the Camp Chase Confederate Cemetery in Columbus, Ohio, you might spot the Lady in Gray.

6. The Stull Cemetery in Kansas City, Missouri, is sometimes fondly referred to as the Gates of Hell, the Cemetery of the Damned, and the Seventh Gate to Hell. The devil himself is said to roam the grounds. Other characters known to hang around this haunt include the devil's child, a boy werewolf, and a witch.

7. Central City, Colorado's Masonic Cemetery is reputed to be haunted by the ghost of a woman who lays flowers on the grave of John Edward Cameron, appearing on April 5 and November 1. Entire groups have seen her.

8. Forest Park Cemetery in Brunswick, New York, is home to many phantoms, including one that can cause a headstone to bleed.

9. Adelaida Cemetery in Paso Robles, California, has an evil poltergeist as well as the ghost of a woman in a long, white nightgown who has been spotted by more than one visitor, usually between the hours of 10 p.m. and midnight on Fridays.

10. New Orleans has no shortage of haunted spots, but the St. Louis Cemetery is arguably one of the most haunted in all of North America. It is said to be home to multiple ghosts, including the Voodoo

Queen, Marie Laveau. Whispers, groans, strange mists, and shadows are all among the regularly experienced phenomena.

11. McConnico Cemetery in Monroe County, Alabama, is haunted by the ghosts of Civil War soldiers.

12. Western Burial Mound in Baltimore, Maryland, may already be on your radar thanks to famous residents Edgar Allan Poe and Francis Scott Key. Visitors have claimed to see Poe, as well as a drunken ghoul and a crazed lunatic.

13. Grand Haven, Michigan's Lake Forest Cemetery has had numerous sightings over the years, including a pale blue man, orbs, mists, black shadows, and the occasional disembodied voice.

Kutná Hora-ble

The Sedlec Ossuary in Kutná Hora, Czech Republic—also known as The Church of Bones—looks like your ordinary, run-of-the-mill medieval church from the outside. But once you step inside, you will be stunned. More than 40,000 skeletons grace this small chapel, including a chandelier said to be made out of every bone in the human body. The ossuary began when the nearby cemetery (striking distance from Sedlec's doors) became too crowded and the bones began, ahem, piling up. In time, the church appointed a local woodworker and artist to arrange the bones. His work includes a coat of arms, the chandelier, and other patterns.

A Haunting in Paris

The Paris catacombs are an eerie place. If it's not enough to imagine walls lined with skulls and vast piles of femurs, consider that to experience them, you must go into the bowels of Paris itself.

Jeff Belanger is no stranger to the world of the paranormal and ghosts. He founded Ghostvillage.com in 1999 and has been a pioneer in the field of a paranormal research ever since. It should come as no surprise to readers that I am a great fan of his work and of the man himself. (He recently completed a trek to the top of Mt. Kilimanjaro!) I am greatly honored to include in this collection his very personal ghost story about one of my favorite European haunts.

The Empire of the Dead

I grew up without ghost experiences. As a kid, I remember other children who would talk about their houses being haunted, and I thought it was interesting and cool, but I personally had never had that kind of experience. When I went away to college and started writing as a journalist, I began searching for ghosts—not for the reason so many do, but because where there are hauntings there is history. I would look for my feature story for Halloween and find an incredible wealth of history. Something I noticed right away was that the more people I interviewed, the more I realized they believed what they were telling me. They truly believed. I don't think any of them were lying.

When I started Ghostvillage.com in 1999, I still had not had a ghost experience myself. This was okay, though, because it allowed me to be the objective journalist—to report the facts and not change the story because of my beliefs. But again, the more I heard other people's stories, the more I came to understand they believed in what they were saying. As a journalist you come to trust your instincts, and with few exceptions, I could tell that the people sharing their stories were telling me the truth.

Everything changed for me in 2003. I went on a business trip to Paris, France. After a long flight, I found myself alone with the day to spend on my own. I decided that instead of the Louvre, I wanted to see the infamous Parisian catacombs. I hopped into a cab and with my rudimentary French managed to get the driver to take me in the right direction. When he dropped me off, I found myself on an ordinary Parisian street: a deli, houses, nothing to indicate a massive underground entrance. I asked a passing woman for directions and she took me to a tiny doorway that opened onto the museum. Inside there was a small entryway where you pay your few euros, and down you go.

I was completely alone. No one else was with me or in the museum, and it was an eerie place. You descend thirty meters below the streets of Paris, where the lighting is low and you can hear the drip of water through the limestone and the crunch of gravel beneath your feet. I am six foot two, and the tunnels are not large. Many times I had to duck to go from passage to passage. And then, I came upon a door. It read:

Arrete!
C'est ici l'empire de la mort.

Stop!
This is the empire of the dead.

Six million skeletons are on the other side of that door: skulls, femurs, bones of all kinds. (I should mention here that as a child I actually had a fear of skeletons: I was convinced I'd be digging in my backyard and would unearth human remains.)

The city of Paris originally laid its cemeteries on the outskirts of town, but as it grew, they began to envelop the city. More and more people, and less and less room for the dead. And so the city came up with this solution: to relocate the bones to an underground resting place, the catacombs.

In order to show respect, these relocated bones were not just piled (although some are in piles) but artfully arranged. You can even find a heart patterned out of skulls. It is awe-inspiring, eerie, macabre, beautiful. Sixty generations of Parisians are here in these tunnels.

As I was continuing down the narrow tunnel, I saw before me the shadow of a man. It went from right to left, then left to right, across the tunnel before me. I froze. Immediately, I tried to rationalize what I had seen: there must be someone else down here with me. The tunnel I was in was no wider than my arms' reach, so no one could have passed by me. I walked a little farther on and could see no side tunnels, no adjoining passage. Was it a trick of the light? A shadow cast by a rat could loom large; but no, the light was at my shoulder. And as I ran through every scenario in my mind, I ran out of every word except one:

Was it a trick of the light?

Ghost.

I had to press on, continue down this passage to where I had seen this shadow. And as I walked closer and closer, all of the experiences I had spent years recording and writing about became so real to me. That thing was there with me. It was in front of me. It was real.

As I continued through the tunnel, I felt a great weight upon me, not one lifted—because I now knew what everyone was talking about. I didn't ask for this experience. And I couldn't deny it. Ghost.

It was a profound experience. Not only was I processing what I had seen, but I had changed. No longer was I this good, objective journalist; I had become a believer. Since that day, I have had a few other experiences (in twenty years of doing this I can count on one hand the number of experiences I've had), but this one has always stayed with me. Life-changing events happen in moments, and those game changers happen when you least expect it. This experience became a defining moment for me and one I will never forget.

—JEFF BELANGER, AS TOLD TO VARLA VENTURA

I was just somebody else, some stranger, and my whole life was a haunted life, the life of a ghost.

—JACK KEROUAC, ON THE ROAD

Rue the Day

Paris, especially the Paris of 1895, makes an exceptional setting for any story of depravity or human horrors. Ralph Adams Cram surely spent time there: a city of romance and outstanding architecture with a seething underbelly and sooty rooftops; finery in the streets and unrefined delights around every corner. Although horror writing was a favorite pastime for him, Cram was actually best known for a different kind of Gothic undertaking. He was a rather famous architect in his day during the Gothic Revival movement at the turn of the twentieth century and was responsible for count-

less famous buildings, in particular cathedrals. Among his structures we find the Calvary Episcopal Church in Pittsburgh, Pennsylvania; The Mather School in Dorchester, Massachusetts; the Public Library in Fall River, Massachusetts; All Saints' Church in Ashmont, Massachusetts; numerous buildings at Princeton University; and dozens of others. In his later career he was a great designer of the Art Deco movement, and one of his buildings of distinction is the Federal Building in Boston. These monumental masterpieces are Cram's living legacy, but as a writer he did afford a certain cult following in his time. In fact, H. P. Lovecraft called his contribution to horror fiction "a memorably potent

degree of vague regional horror through subtleties of atmosphere and description." (Trust me, from Lovecraft, that is a compliment.)

As with any classic tale of terror, you will find here the suspenseful setting, the requisite dead relative, the abandoned mysterious residence. Cram's architectural acumen comes across in his detailed descriptions of the buildings inside and out. Without giving too much away, the secret chamber (it's inevitable, isn't it?) graced with a goddess and a pentagram is described down to the sheen of the paint on the wall. These details only add to the credibility, the *possibility*, of this story. While I recommend reading this tucked beneath the brocade covers in a boutique Parisian hotel room, I implore you to avoid perusing it should a storm be approaching. It would not do to be partway through and be startled suddenly by the rumble of thunder or the blacking out of the lights. It would not do at all.

No. 252 Rue M. le Prince

When in May, 1886, I found myself at last in Paris, I naturally determined to throw myself on the charity of an old chum of mine, Eugene Marie d'Ardeche, who had forsaken Boston a year or more ago on receiving word of the death of an aunt who had left him such property as she possessed. I fancy this windfall surprised him not a little, for the relations between the aunt and nephew had never been cordial, judging from Eugene's remarks touching the lady, who was, it seems, a more or less wicked and witch-like old person, with a penchant for black magic, at least such was the common report.

Why she should leave all her property to d'Ardeche, no one could tell, unless it was that she felt his rather hobbledehoy tendencies towards Buddhism and occultism might some day lead him to her own unhallowed height of questionable illumination. To be sure d'Ardeche reviled her as a bad old woman, being himself in that state of enthusiastic exaltation which sometimes accompanies a boyish fancy for occultism; but in spite of his distant and repellent attitude, Mlle. Blaye de Tartas made him her sole heir, to the violent wrath of a questionable old party known to infamy as the Sar Torrevieja, the "King of the Sorcerers." This malevolent

old portent, whose gray and crafty face was often seen in the Rue M. le Prince during the life of Mlle. de Tartas had, it seems, fully expected to enjoy her small wealth after her death; and when it appeared that she had left him only the contents of the gloomy old house in the Quartier Latin, giving the house itself and all else of which she died possessed to her nephew in America, the Sar proceeded to remove everything from the place, and then to curse it elaborately and comprehensively, together with all those who should ever dwell therein.

Whereupon he disappeared.

This final episode was the last word I receive from Eugene, but I knew the number of the house, 252 Rue M. le Prince. So, after a day or two given to a first cursory survey of Paris, I started across the Seine to find Eugene and compel him to do the honors of the city.

Every one who knows the Latin Quarter knows the Rue M. le Prince, running up the hill towards the Garden of the Luxembourg. It is full of queer houses and odd corners,—or was in '86,—and certainly No. 252 was, when I found it, quite as queer as any. It was nothing but a doorway, a black arch of old stone between and under two new houses painted yellow. The effect of this bit of seventeenth-century masonry, with its dirty old doors, and rusty broken lantern sticking gaunt and grim out over the narrow sidewalk, was, in its frame of fresh plaster, sinister in the extreme.

I wondered if I had made a mistake in the number; it was quite evident that no one lived behind those cobwebs. I went into the doorway of one of the new hôtels and interviewed the concierge.

No, M. d'Ardeche did not live there, though to be sure he owned the mansion; he himself resided in Meudon, in the country house of the late Mlle. de Tartas. Would Monsieur like the number and the street?

Monsieur would like them extremely, so I took the card that the concierge wrote for me, and forthwith started for the river, in order that I might take a steamboat for Meudon. By one of those coincidences which happen so often, being quite inexplicable, I had not gone twenty paces down the street before I ran directly into the arms of Eugene d'Ardeche. In three minutes we were sitting in the queer little garden of the Chien Bleu, drinking vermouth and absinthe, and talking it all over.

"You do not live in your aunt's house?" I said at last, interrogatively.

"No, but if this sort of thing keeps on I shall have to. I like Meudon much better, and the house is perfect, all furnished, and nothing in it newer than the last century. You must come out with me to-night and see it. I have got a jolly room fixed up for my Buddha. But there is something wrong with this house opposite. I can't keep a tenant in it,— not four days. I have had three, all within six months, but the stories have gone around and a man would as soon think of hiring the Cour des Comptes to live in as No. 252. It is notorious. The fact is, it is haunted the worst way."

I laughed and ordered more vermouth.

"That is all right. It is haunted all the same, or enough to keep it empty, and the funny part is that no one knows how it is haunted. Nothing is ever seen, nothing heard. As far as I can find out, people just have the horrors there, and have them so bad they have to go to the hospital afterwards. I have one ex-tenant in the Bicêtre now. So the house stands empty, and as it covers considerable ground and is taxed for a lot, I don't know what to do about it. I think I'll either give it to that child of sin, Torrevieja, or else go and live in it myself. I shouldn't mind the ghosts, I am sure."

"Did you ever stay there?"

"No, but I have always intended to, and in fact I came up here to-day to see a couple of rake-hell fellows I know, Fargeau and Duchesne, doctors in the Clinical Hospital beyond here, up by the Parc Mont Souris. They promised that they would spend the night with me some time in my aunt's house,—which is called around here, you must know, 'la Bouche d'Enfer,'—and I thought perhaps they would make it this week, if they can get off duty. Come up with me while I see them, and then we can go across the river to Véfour's and have some luncheon, you can get your things at the Chatham, and we will go out to Meudon, where of course you will spend the night with me."

The plan suited me perfectly, so we went up to the hospital, found Fargeau, who declared that he and Duchesne were ready for anything, the nearer the real "bouche d'enfer" the better; that the following Thursday they would both be off duty for the night, and that on that day they would join in an attempt to outwit the devil and clear up the mystery of No. 252.

"Does M. l'Américain go with us?" asked Fargeau.

"Why of course," I replied, "I intend to go, and you must not refuse me, d'Ardeche; I decline to be put off. Here is a chance for you to do the honors of your city in a manner which is faultless. Show me a real live ghost, and I will forgive Paris for having lost the Jardin Mabille."

So it was settled.

Later we went down to Meudon and ate dinner in the terrace room of the villa, which was all that d'Ardeche had said, and more, so utterly was its atmosphere that of the seventeenth century. At dinner Eugene told me more about his late aunt, and the queer goings on in the old house.

Mlle. Blaye lived, it seems, all alone, except for one female servant of her own age; a severe, taciturn creature, with massive Breton features and a Breton tongue, whenever she vouchsafed to use it. No one ever was seen to enter the door of No. 252 except Jeanne the servant and the Sar Torrevieja, the latter coming constantly from none knew whither, and always entering, never leaving. Indeed, the neighbors, who for eleven years had watched the old sorcerer sidle crab-wise up to the bell almost every day, declared vociferously that never had he been seen to leave the house. Once, when they decided to keep absolute guard, the watcher, none other than Maître Garceau of the Chien Bleu, after keeping his eyes fixed on the door from ten o'clock one morning when the Sar arrived until four in the afternoon, during which time the door was unopened (he knew this, for had he not gummed a ten-centime stamp over the joint and was not the stamp unbroken) nearly fell down when the sinister figure of Torrevieja slid wickedly by him with a dry "Pardon, Monsieur!" and disappeared again through the black doorway.

This was curious, for No. 252 was entirely surrounded by houses, its only windows opening on a courtyard into which no eye could look from the hôtels of the Rue M. le Prince and the Rue de l'Ecole, and the mystery was one of the choice possessions of the Latin Quarter.

Once a year the austerity of the place was broken, and the denizens of the whole quarter stood open-mouthed watching many carriages drive up to No. 252, many of them private, not a few with crests on the door panels, from all of them descending veiled female figures and men with coat collars turned up. Then followed curious sounds of music from within, and those whose houses joined the blank walls of No. 252 became for the moment popular, for by placing the ear against the wall strange music could distinctly be heard, and the sound of monotonous chanting voices now and then. By dawn the last guest would have departed, and for another year the hôtel of Mlle. de Tartas was ominously silent.

Eugene declared that he believed it was a celebration of "Walpurgisnacht," and certainly appearances favored such a fancy.

"A queer thing about the whole affair is," he said, "the fact that every one in the street swears that about a month ago, while I was out in Concarneau for a visit, the music and voices were heard again, just as when my revered aunt was in the flesh. The house was perfectly empty, as I tell you, so it is quite possible that the good people were enjoying an hallucination."

I must acknowledge that these stories did not reassure me; in fact, as Thursday came near, I began to regret a little my determination to spend the night in the house. I was too vain to back down, however, and the perfect coolness of the two doctors, who ran down Tuesday to Meudon to make a few arrangements, caused me to swear that I would die of fright before I would flinch. I suppose I believed more or less in ghosts, I am sure now that I am older I believe in them, there are in fact few things I can not believe. Two or three inexplicable things had happened to me, and, although this was before my adventure with Rendel in Pæstum, I had a strong predisposition to believe some things that I could not explain, wherein I was out of sympathy with the age.

Well, to come to the memorable night of the twelfth of June, we had made our preparations, and after depositing a big bag inside the doors of No. 252, went across to the Chien Bleu, where Fargeau and Duchesne turned up promptly, and we sat down to the best dinner Père Garceau could create.

I remember I hardly felt that the conversation was in good taste. It began with various stories of Indian fakirs and Oriental jugglery, matters in which Eugene was curiously well read, swerved to the horrors of the great Sepoy mutiny, and thus to reminiscences of the dissecting-room. By this time we had drunk more or less, and Duchesne launched into a photographic and Zolaesque account of the only time (as he said) when he was possessed of the panic of fear; namely, one night many years ago, when he was locked by accident into the dissecting-room of the Loucine, together with several cadavers of a rather unpleasant nature. I ventured to protest mildly against the choice of subjects, the result being a perfect carnival of horrors, so that when we finally drank our last crème de cacao and started for "la Bouche d'Enfer," my nerves were in a somewhat rocky condition.

It was just ten o'clock when we came into the street. A hot dead wind drifted in great puffs through the city, and ragged masses of vapor swept the purple sky; an unsavory night altogether, one of those nights of hopeless lassitude when one feels, if one is at home, like doing nothing but drink mint juleps and smoke cigarettes.

Eugene opened the creaking door, and tried to light one of the lanterns; but the gusty wind blew out every match, and we finally had to close the outer doors before we could get a light. At last we had all the lanterns going, and I began to look around curiously. We were in a long, vaulted passage, partly carriageway, partly footpath, perfectly bare but for the street refuse which had drifted in with eddying winds. Beyond lay the courtyard, a curious place rendered more curious still by the fitful moonlight and the flashing of four dark lanterns. The place had evidently been once a most noble palace. Opposite rose the oldest portion, a three-story wall of the time of Francis I., with a great wisteria vine covering half. The wings on either side were more modern, seventeenth century, and ugly, while towards the street was nothing but a flat unbroken wall.

The great bare court, littered with bits of paper blown in by the wind, fragments of packing cases, and straw, mysterious with flashing lights and flaunting shadows, while low masses of torn vapor drifted overhead, hiding, then revealing the stars, and all in absolute silence, not even the sounds of the streets entering this prison-like place, was weird and uncanny in the extreme. I must confess that already I began to feel a slight disposition towards the horrors, but with that curious inconsequence which so often happens in the case of those who are deliberately growing scared, I could think of nothing more reassuring than those delicious verses of Lewis Carroll's:—

"Just the place for a Snark! I have said it twice, That alone should encourage the crew. Just the place for a Snark! I have said it thrice, What I tell you three times is true,"—which kept repeating themselves over and over in my brain with feverish insistence.

Even the medical students had stopped their chaffing, and were studying the surroundings gravely.

"There is one thing certain," said Fargeau, "anything might have happened here without the slightest chance of discovery. Did ever you see such a perfect place for lawlessness?"

"And anything might happen here now, with the same certainty of impunity," continued Duchesne, lighting his pipe, the snap of the match making us all start. "D'Ardeche, your lamented relative was certainly well fixed; she had full scope here for her traditional experiments in demonology."

"Curse me if I don't believe that those same traditions were more or less founded on fact," said Eugene. "I never saw this court under these conditions before, but I could believe anything now. What's that!"

"Nothing but a door slamming," said Duchesne, loudly.

> **"Well, I wish doors wouldn't slam in houses that have been empty eleven months."**

"Well, I wish doors wouldn't slam in houses that have been empty eleven months."

"It is irritating," and Duchesne slipped his arm through mine; "but we must take things as they come. Remember we have to deal not only with the spectral lumber left here by your scarlet aunt, but as well with the supererogatory curse of that hell-cat Torrevieja. Come on! let's get inside before the hour arrives for the sheeted dead to squeak and gibber in these lonely halls. Light your pipes, your tobacco is a sure protection against 'your whoreson dead bodies'; light up and move on."

We opened the hall door and entered a vaulted stone vestibule, full of dust, and cobwebby.

"There is nothing on this floor," said Eugene, "except servants' rooms and offices, and I don't believe there is anything wrong with them. I never heard that there was, any way. Let's go up stairs."

So far as we could see, the house was apparently perfectly uninteresting inside, all eighteenth-century work, the façade of the main building being, with the vestibule, the only portion of the Francis I. work.

"The place was burned during the Terror," said Eugene, "for my great-uncle, from whom Mlle. de Tartas inherited it, was a good and true Royalist; he went to Spain after the Revolution, and did not come back until the accession of Charles X., when he restored the house, and then died, enormously old. This explains why it is all so new."

The old Spanish sorcerer to whom Mlle. de Tartas had left her personal property had done his work thoroughly. The house was absolutely empty, even the wardrobes and bookcases built in had been carried away; we went through room after room, finding all absolutely dismantled, only the windows and doors with their casings, the parquet floors, and the florid Renaissance mantels remaining.

"I feel better," remarked Fargeau. "The house may be haunted, but it don't look it, certainly; it is the most respectable place imaginable."

"Just you wait," replied Eugene. "These are only the state apartments, which my aunt seldom used, except, perhaps, on her annual 'Walpurgisnacht.' Come up stairs and I will show you a better mise en scène."

On this floor, the rooms fronting the court, the sleeping-rooms, were quite small,—("They are the bad rooms all the same," said Eugene,)—four of them, all just as ordinary in appearance as those below. A corridor ran behind them connecting with the wing corridor, and from this opened a door, unlike any of the other doors in that it was covered with green baize, somewhat moth-eaten. Eugene selected a key from the bunch he carried, unlocked the door, and with some difficulty forced it to swing inward; it was as heavy as the door of a safe.

> "We are now," he said, "on the very threshold of hell itself . . ."

"We are now," he said, "on the very threshold of hell itself; these rooms in here were my scarlet aunt's unholy of unholies. I never let them with the rest of the house, but keep them as a curiosity. I only wish Torrevieja had kept out; as it was, he looted them, as he did the rest of the house, and nothing is left but the walls and ceiling and floor. They are something, however, and may suggest what the former condition must have been. Tremble and enter."

The first apartment was a kind of anteroom, a cube of perhaps twenty feet each way, without windows, and with no doors except that by which we entered and another to the right. Walls, floor, and ceiling were covered with a black lacquer, brilliantly polished, that flashed the light of our lanterns in a thousand intricate reflections. It was like the inside of an enormous Japanese box, and about as empty. From this we passed to another room, and here we nearly dropped our lanterns. The room was circular, thirty feet or so in diameter, covered by a hemispherical dome; walls and ceiling were dark blue, spotted with gold stars; and reaching from floor to floor across the dome stretched a colossal figure in red lacquer of a nude woman kneeling, her legs reaching out along the floor on either side, her head touching the lintel of the door through which we had entered, her arms forming its sides, with the fore arms extended and stretching along the walls until they met the long feet. The most astounding, misshapen, absolutely terrifying thing, I think, I ever saw. From the navel hung a great white object, like the traditional roe's egg of the Arabian Nights. The floor was of red lacquer, and in it was inlaid a pentagram the size of

> **The most astounding, misshapen, absolutely terrifying thing, I think, I ever saw.**

the room, made of wide strips of brass. In the centre of this pentagram was a circular disk of black stone, slightly saucer-shaped, with a small outlet in the middle.

The effect of the room was simply crushing, with this gigantic red figure crouched over it all, the staring eyes fixed on one, no matter what his position. None of us spoke, so oppressive was the whole thing.

The third room was like the first in dimensions, but instead of being black it was entirely sheathed with plates of brass, walls, ceiling, and floor,—tarnished now, and turning green, but still brilliant under the lantern light. In the middle stood an oblong altar of porphyry, its longer dimensions on the axis of the suite of rooms, and at one end, opposite the range of doors, a pedestal of black basalt.

This was all. Three rooms, stranger than these, even in their emptiness, it would be hard to imagine. In Egypt, in India, they would not be entirely out of place, but here in Paris, in a commonplace hôtel, in the Rue M. le Prince, they were incredible.

We retraced our steps, Eugene closed the iron door with its baize covering, and we went into one of the front chambers and sat down, looking at each other.

"Nice party, your aunt," said Fargeau. "Nice old party, with amiable tastes; I am glad we are not to spend the night in those rooms."

"What do you suppose she did there?" inquired Duchesne. "I know more or less about black art, but that series of rooms is too much for me."

"My impression is," said d'Ardeche, "that the brazen room was a kind of sanctuary containing some image or other on the basalt base, while the stone in front was really an altar,—what the nature of the sacrifice might be I don't even guess. The round room may have been used for invocations and incantations. The pentagram looks like it. Any way it is all just about as queer and fin de siècle as I can well imagine. Look here, it is nearly twelve, let's dispose of ourselves, if we are going to hunt this thing down."

The four chambers on this floor of the old house were those said to be haunted, the wings being quite innocent, and, so far as we knew, the floors below. It was arranged that we should each occupy a room, leaving the doors open with the lights burning, and at the slightest cry or knock we were all to rush at once to the room from which the warning sound might come. There was no communication between the rooms to be sure, but, as the doors all opened into the corridor, every sound was plainly audible.

The last room fell to me, and I looked it over carefully.

It seemed innocent enough, a commonplace, square, rather lofty Parisian sleeping-room, finished in wood painted white, with a small marble mantel, a dusty floor of inlaid maple and cherry, walls hung with an ordinary French paper, apparently quite new, and two deeply embrasured windows looking out on the court.

I opened the swinging sash with some trouble, and sat down in the window seat with my lantern beside me trained on the only door, which gave on the corridor.

The wind had gone down, and it was very still without,—still and hot. The masses of luminous vapor were gathering thickly overhead, no longer urged by the gusty wind. The great masses of rank wisteria leaves, with here and there a second blossoming of purple flowers, hung dead over the window in the sluggish air. Across the roofs I could hear the sound of a belated fiacre in the streets below. I filled my pipe again and waited.

For a time the voices of the men in the other rooms were a companionship, and at first I shouted to them now and then, but my voice echoed rather unpleasantly through the long corridors, and had a suggestive way of reverberating around the left wing beside me, and coming out at a broken window at its extremity like the voice of another man. I soon gave up my attempts at conversation, and devoted myself to the task of keeping awake.

It was not easy; why did I eat that lettuce salad at Père Garceau's? I should have known better. It was making me irresistibly sleepy, and wakefulness was absolutely necessary. It was certainly gratifying to know that I could sleep, that my courage was by me to that extent, but in the interests of science I must keep awake. But almost never, it seemed, had sleep looked so desirable. Half a hundred times, nearly, I would doze for an instant, only to awake with a start, and find my pipe gone out. Nor did the exertion of relighting it pull me together. I struck my match mechanically, and with the first puff dropped off again. It was most vexing. I got up and walked around the room. It was most annoying. My cramped position had almost put both my legs to sleep. I could hardly stand. I felt numb, as though with cold. There was no longer any sound from the other rooms, nor from without. I sank down in my window seat. How dark it was growing! I turned up the lantern. That pipe again, how obstinately it kept going out! and my last match was gone. The lantern, too, was that going out? I lifted my hand to turn it up again. It felt like lead, and fell beside me.

Then I awoke,—absolutely. I remembered the story of "The Haunters and the Haunted." This was the Horror. I tried to rise, to cry out. My body was like lead, my tongue was paralyzed. I could hardly move my eyes. And the light was going out. There was no question about that. Darker and darker yet; little by little the pattern of the paper was swallowed up in the advancing night. A prickling numbness gathered in every nerve, my

This was the Horror. I tried to rise, to cry out. My body was like lead, my tongue was paralyzed.

right arm slipped without feeling from my lap to my side, and I could not raise it,—it swung helpless. A thin, keen humming began in my head, like the cicadas on a hillside in September. The darkness was coming fast.

Yes, this was it. Something was subjecting me, body and mind, to slow paralysis. Physically I was already dead. If I could only hold my mind, my consciousness, I might still be safe, but could I? Could I resist the mad horror of this silence, the deepening dark, the creeping numbness? I knew that, like the man in the ghost story, my only safety lay here.

It had come at last. My body was dead, I could no longer move my eyes. They were fixed in that last look on the place where the door had been, now only a deepening of the dark.

Utter night: the last flicker of the lantern was gone. I sat and waited; my mind was still keen, but how long would it last? There was a limit even to the endurance of the utter panic of fear.

Then the end began. In the velvet blackness came two white eyes, milky, opalescent, small, far away,— awful eyes, like a dead dream. More beautiful than I can describe, the flakes of white flame moving from the perimeter inward, disappearing in the centre, like a never ending flow of opal water into a circular tunnel. I could not have moved my eyes had I possessed the power: they devoured the fearful, beautiful things that grew slowly, slowly larger, fixed on me, advancing, growing more beautiful, the white flakes of light sweeping more swiftly into the blazing vortices, the awful fascination deepening in its insane intensity as the white, vibrating eyes grew nearer, larger.

Like a hideous and implacable engine of death the eyes of the unknown Horror swelled and expanded until they were close before me, enormous, terrible, and I felt a slow, cold, wet breath propelled with mechanical regularity against my face, enveloping me in its fetid mist, in its charnel-house deadliness.

With ordinary fear goes always a physical terror, but with me in the presence of this unspeakable Thing was only the utter and awful terror of the mind, the mad fear of a prolonged and ghostly nightmare. Again and again I tried to shriek, to make some noise, but physically I was utterly dead. I could only feel myself go mad with the terror of hideous death. The eyes were close on

me,—their movement so swift that they seemed to be but palpitating flames, the dead breath was around me like the depths of the deepest sea.

Suddenly a wet, icy mouth, like that of a dead cuttle-fish, shapeless, jelly-like, fell over mine. The horror began slowly to draw my life from me, but, as enormous and shuddering folds of palpitating jelly swept sinuously around me, my will came back, my body awoke with the reaction of final fear, and I closed with the nameless death that enfolded me.

What was it that I was fighting? My arms sunk through the unresisting mass that was turning me to ice. Moment by moment new folds of cold jelly swept round me, crushing me with the force of Titans. I fought to wrest my mouth from this awful Thing that sealed it, but, if ever I succeeded and caught a single breath, the wet, sucking mass closed over my face again before I could cry out. I think I fought for hours, desperately, insanely, in a silence that was more hideous than any sound,—fought until I felt final death at hand, until the memory of all my

> **Suddenly a wet, icy mouth, like that of a dead cuttle-fish, shapeless, jelly-like, fell over mine.**

life rushed over me like a flood, until I no longer had strength to wrench my face from that hellish succubus, until with a last mechanical struggle I fell and yielded to death.

Then I heard a voice say, "If he is dead, I can never forgive myself; I was to blame."

Another replied, "He is not dead, I know we can save him if only we reach the hospital in time. Drive like hell, cocher! twenty francs for you, if you get there in three minutes."

Then there was night again, and nothingness, until I suddenly awoke and stared around. I lay in a hospital ward, very white and sunny, some yellow fleurs-de-lis stood beside the head of the pallet, and a tall sister of mercy sat by my side.

To tell the story in a few words, I was in the Hôtel Dieu, where the men had taken me that fearful night of the twelfth of June. I asked for Fargeau or Duchesne, and by and by the latter came, and sitting beside the bed told me all that I did not know.

It seems that they had sat, each in his room, hour after hour, hearing nothing, very much bored, and disappointed. Soon after two o'clock Fargeau, who was in the next room, called to me to ask if I was awake.

I gave no reply, and, after shouting once or twice, he took his lantern and came to investigate. The door was locked on the inside! He instantly called d'Ardeche and Duchesne, and together they hurled themselves against the door. It resisted. Within they could hear irregular footsteps dashing here and there, with heavy breathing. Although frozen with terror, they fought to destroy the door and finally succeeded by using a great slab of marble that formed the shelf of the mantel in Fargeau's room. As the door crashed in, they were suddenly hurled back against the walls of the corridor, as though by an explosion, the lanterns were extinguished, and they found themselves in utter silence and darkness.

As soon as they recovered from the shock, they leaped into the room and fell over my body in the middle of the floor. They lighted one of the lanterns, and saw the strangest sight that can be imagined. The floor and walls to the height of about six feet were running with something that seemed like stagnant water, thick, glutinous, sickening. As for me, I was drenched with the same cursed liquid. The odor of musk was nauseating. They dragged me away, stripped off my clothing, wrapped me in their coats, and hurried to the hospital, thinking me perhaps dead. Soon after sunrise d'Ardeche left the hospital, being assured that I was in a fair way to recovery, with time, and with Fargeau went up to examine by daylight the traces of the adventure that was so nearly fatal. They were too late. Fire engines were coming down the street as they passed the Académie. A neighbor rushed up to d'Ardeche: "O Monsieur! what misfortune, yet what fortune! It is true la Bouche d'Enfer—I beg pardon, the residence of the lamented Mlle. de Tartas,—was burned, but not wholly, only the ancient building. The wings were saved, and for that great credit is due the brave firemen. Monsieur will remember them, no doubt."

It was quite true. Whether a forgotten lantern, overturned in the excitement, had done the work, or whether the origin of the fire was more supernatural,

it was certain that "the Mouth of Hell" was no more. A last engine was pumping slowly as d'Ardeche came up; half a dozen limp, and one distended, hose stretched through the porte cochère, and within only the façade of Francis I. remained, draped still with the black stems of the wisteria. Beyond lay a great vacancy, where thin smoke was rising slowly. Every floor was gone, and the strange halls of Mlle. Blaye de Tartas were only a memory.

With d'Ardeche I visited the place last year, but in the stead of the ancient walls was then only a new and ordinary building, fresh and respectable; yet the wonderful stories of the old Bouche d'Enfer still lingered in the quarter, and will hold there, I do not doubt, until the Day of Judgment.

—RALPH ADAMS CRAM, *BLACK SPIRITS AND WHITE*

American Ghost Story

[There is] the constant appearance, in American communities, of ghosts of the old-fashioned sort. Especially in the New England states, which are notable for their enlightenment, are ghost-stories still frequent—such as that of the haunted school-house at Newburyport, Mass., where a disembodied spirit related its own murder; of the ghost of New Bedford, which struck a visitor in the face, so that he yet bears the marks of the blow; of the haunted house at Cambridge, in the classic shadow of Harvard College. It is actually on record in the last-named case, that the house fell to decay on account of its ghastly reputation, as no one would live in it; that a tenant who ventured to occupy it in 1877 was disturbed by the spirit of a murdered girl who said her mortal bones were buried in his cellar; and that a party of men actually dug all night in that cellar in search of those bones, while the ghost waltzed in a chamber overhead. The more common form of spirit peculiar to our time appears constantly in various parts of the country; it is continually turning up in the American newspapers, rapping on walls, throwing stones, tipping over tables, etc. 'Mediums' of every grade of shrewdness and stupidity, and widely differing degrees of education and ignorance, flourish abundantly.

> **A party of men actually dug all night in that cellar in search of those bones, while the ghost waltzed in a chamber overhead.**

—WILLIAM WIRT SIKES, *BRITISH GOBLINS*

"Other cities resemble all the birds and beasts and fishes whose appetites and digestions are normal. Paris alone is the analogical apotheosis of the octopus. Product of centralization carried to an ad absurdum, it fairly represents the devil fish; and in no respects is the resemblance more curious than in the similarity of the digestive apparatus."

—BRAM STOKER, "BURIAL OF RATS"

Six Signs of a Haunting

Here are six signs your house might be haunted (although I'm not going to lie, many of these may indicate the presence of a house brownie or hobgoblin).

1. Pets bark, growl, or hiss at seemingly out-of-place times, in particular at empty corners or interior doorways.

2. You or other members of your house have repeated nightmares.

3. Objects disappear (again, could be a fairy trick) but then reappear again at a later time in a strange place.

4. Electrical appliances turn on or off by themselves and lights flicker. Toilets flush or faucets turn on or off on their own.

5. You notice inexplicable cold drafts or cold spots.

6. You frequently hear footsteps, tappings on walls or windows, and other sounds that cannot be attributed to people or pets.

Chapter 3

Ouija Look at That

Paranormal Parlor Games, Séances,
Psychic Arts, and Afterlife Novels

And here you must on no pretence
    Make the first observation.
Wait for the Victim to commence:
    No Ghost of any common sense
    Begins a conversation.

—LEWIS CARROLL, CANTO II: HYS FYVE
RULES FROM "PHANTASMAGORIA"

Spirited Away

I was probably seven years old the first time I dabbled
in the fine art of metaphysics. A mysterious gift arrived
under the Christmas tree, wrapped in bright red paper
and suspiciously like the shape of a Monopoly board.
My sister and I were gleeful to discover that it was not
the suspected Monopoly board at all, but instead a different board game: the Ouija board. While this may not
seem the typical gift for the average kid, bear in mind it
was the 1980s and white blazers and mullets were also
in fashion—I mean, it was a different era. And consider
also that our holiday tree was bedecked with jack-o'-
lantern lights alongside candy canes and a few leftover
Halloween skeletons.

We couldn't wait to get our tiny hands on this parlor
game, and it didn't take long before it became a regular

ritual for the two of us with the occasional overseeing by my mom.

The following spring, after passing a winter using the Ouija board without much paranormal activity, we discovered something that set a series of creepy communications in motion. While scrambling after our little brother through the woods, we happened upon an old grave that belonged to a young pioneer girl who had died at the age of eight, sometime in the late 1800s. (This seems like the groundwork for a horror story, I know, but it is a true tale of terror from my own childhood.) We lived several miles from the nearest town in the remote foothills of California and were accustomed

to 1) clambering around in the woods and 2) exploring spooky pioneer cemeteries. Still, even to us, that one lone grave in the woods, and the fact that it belonged to a kid close to our own ages, upped the freaky quotient to a level that haunted us as dark settled that night.

> **I will never forget the eerie sensation when the marker began to move on its own.**

It could have been the power of suggestion, the sad grave, and its spirit lodged into our subconscious minds, but within a week the ghost of the girl, whom I'll call Jenny, started making an appearance on our spirit-board. I will never forget the eerie sensation when the marker began to move on its own. Wide-eyed and goosebumped, my sister and I looked at each other and then promptly accused one another of pushing the planchette from letter to letter. I knew I hadn't moved it, and she swore she hadn't either.

That we'd made contact with the Other Side remains a certainty in my mind to this day. The significance of what was actually happening was a little lost on us at the time, being as young as we were. (Children have a natural telepathy that an adult mind often suppresses.)

The gravity of the situation was not lost on my mother, however. When we recounted the information we were beginning to receive from young Jenny, Mom marched into my room and snatched up the board (to this day she won't say if she kept it or threw it out!), muttering something about opening a portal we were not able to close. We wanted to know what happened to this young ghost. Why was she buried in a lone grave? Did she live on that property? How did she die? To our curious minds the interruption of this great mystery was a disappointment we would not soon forget (and still have not solved).

Apparently, my mother was not so concerned that we would be communicating with the young ghost (there is something sweet about it, really) but rather that we had actually made contact with a darker entity posing as the ghost of Lil' Jenny, in order to gain control over our own mortal, vulnerable, young minds. (Okay, this is probably sounding crazy to some of you, especially if your mom was the type who shuttled you to ballet or tennis lessons and baked pies for the bake sale. Mine was busy doing battle with dark forces, and hey, that's what made Varla, Varla.) And since this time, as I have wandered my own crooked path, I have met many a seasoned witch, well-worn ghost hunter, and

Spiritualist alike who cringed at the very mention of the world of Ouija. In the following pages I will share with you a few of my favorite spirit-board stories, both historic and recent. Is the Ouija board a "thing-of-evil," or are we just ascribing darkness to something we might never be able to drag out into the light?

Say My Name

Some say the word *Ouija* is derived from "oui," meaning "yes" in French, and "ja," meaning "yes" in many Scandinavian languages. Other stories say that the word came to inventor Charles Kennard during a séance and that it means "good luck" in the ancient Egyptian language. The term *Ouija* can refer, of course, to what is also called a spirit-board: any surface painted with numbers, letters, and symbols used as a means to communicate with the dead. The Ouija Board, however, was patented by Parker Brothers back in 1920. Chances are, if you've played with a Ouija Board, you've scryed right over those little trademarks that prove it.

But long before the paranormal parlor games that gained popularity in Victorian times, scrying was considered a legit means of communicating with gods and goddesses. In fact, whoever was able to do the communing was a revered and important member of the

society. Where today we might see a charlatan, people once saw and sought counsel with the town psychic, medium, healer, or witch (which might have been the same person!).

Anyone who has laid fingers to planchette to spiritboard can attest that it's not exactly a fast process. Usually, in the midst of an impromptu séance, the tension and fear in the room lend themselves nicely to the slow slide of the pointer to each letter. But imagine, if you will, "writing" an entire novel with nothing more than the Ouija board to guide you, letter by letter.

Emily Grant Hutchings (1869–?) did just that, or so she claimed. Her novel, *Jap Herron*, published in 1917 (though it barely saw the light of day), was purported to be not by Mrs. Hutchings at all, but rather was dictated to her by the ghost of Samuel Clemens, aka Mark Twain. With a spirit-board, a medium, and a handy husband taking notes, the entire lengthy novel was—as Hutchings claimed—the lost and last great work of Mark Twain himself.

Consider that if you were a woman "coming of age" at the turn of the twentieth century, you had somewhat limited options for what you could do with your life. You could become a school marm or perhaps join a convent; pursue prostitution and other leisure arts such as gambling and bartending; you could marry and toil (though if you married up, others would toil for you).

There was also one other particular way in which women could forge a viable income but still be considered "respectable" members of society: learn the psychic arts.

In 1915 Emily Grant Hutchings began receiving messages from Mark Twain via the Ouija board. She was compelled to write the novel down and then find a publisher. In her introduction to this channeled novel *Jap Herron,* Hutchings lays out the details of this fascinating paranormal parlor-game-turned-type-writer. Mrs. Hutchings, a medium named Mrs. Hays, who acted as the conduit, and Hutchings's husband worked tirelessly to transcribe and then edit this and two other works of fiction by the then-dead great American novelist. They cleverly modified the Ouija board to include punctuation marks. Hutchings recalls a fascinating exchange with the spirit of Twain and his own typos: Twain's ghost repeatedly used the comma instead of the apostrophe until Hutchings's husband fixed the board again with a bit of India ink, customized to Twain's (and his wife's) liking.

Jap Herron was originally published in 1917 by a book dealer named Mitchell Kennerley and became a controversial affair when Mark Twain's daughter, Clara Clemens, and his publisher (Harper and Brothers) caught wind of it. They promptly sued to halt the publication. Though the book had been published, the lawsuit never went to court—Hutchings and Kennerley agreed to withdraw the book and cease all distribution. Nonetheless, a few copies survived over the last nearly hundred years—and happily have been resurrected for the electronic age.

The quirky thing is that the conversations, quotes, and novel itself are decidedly Twain. The very tone and setting seem classic. Of course many, many skeptics declare there is no real claim here, that the Hutchings and Mrs. Hays were charlatans trying only to sell the novel of a failed author on speculation (Emily had made attempts to publish longer works of her own fiction to no avail). Did the ghost of Mark Twain choose Emily Hutchings to be his scribe and put forth the works he'd yet to write? Or was it all a hoax, a ruse to get her name in print? In addition, there is some evidence that Twain and Hutchings did have some brief correspondence and probably met at least once in person. It appears that young Hutchings was an ambitious writer and sought the counsel of Twain (whose address she obtained through mutual acquaintances).

Here's a little excerpt from that introduction she called "The Coming of 'Jap Herron'":

On the afternoon of the second Thursday in March, 1916, I responded to an invitation to the regular meeting of a small psychical research society. There was to be a lecture on cosmic relations, and the hostess for the afternoon, whom I had met twice socially, thought I might be interested, my name having appeared in connection with a recently detailed series of psychic experiments. To all those present, with the exception of the hostess, I was a total stranger. I learned, with some surprise, that these men and women had been meeting, with an occasional break of a few months, for more than five years. The record of these meetings filled several type-written volumes.

When word came that the lecturer was unavoidably detained, the hostess requested Mrs. Lola V. Hays to entertain the members and guests by a demonstration of her ability to transmit spirit messages by means of a planchette and a lettered board. The apparatus was familiar to me; but the outcome of that afternoon's experience revealed a new use for the transmission board. After several messages, more or less personal, had been spelled out, the pointer of the planchette traced the words:

"Samuel L. Clemens, lazy Sam." There was a long pause, and then: "Well, why don't some of you say something?"

I was born in Hannibal, and my pulses quickened. I wanted to put a host of questions to the greatest humorist and the greatest philosopher of modern times; but I was an outsider, unacquainted with the usages of the club, and I remained silent while the planchette continued:

"Say, folks, don't knock my memoirs too hard. They were written when Mark Twain was dead to all sense of decency. When brains are soft, the method should be anesthesia."

Not one of those present had read Mark Twain's memoirs, and the plaint fell upon barren soil. The arrival of the lecturer prevented further confession from the unseen communicant; but I was so deeply impressed that I begged my hostess to permit me to come again. For my benefit a meeting was arranged at which there was no lecturer, and I was asked to sit for the first time with Mrs. Hays.

In my former psychic investigation, it had been my habit to pronounce the letters as the pointer of the planchette indicated them, and Mrs. Hays urged me to render the same service when I sat with her, because she never permitted herself to look at the board, fearing that her own mind would interfere with the transmission. Scarcely had our finger-tips touched the planchette when it darted to the letters which spelled the words:

"I tried to write a romance once, and the little wife laughed at it. I still think it is good stuff and I want it written. The plot is simple. You'd best skeletonize the plot. Solly Jenks, Hiram Wall—young men. Time, before the Civil War."

Then the outline of a typical Mark Twain story came in short, explosive sentences. It was entitled, "Up the Furrow to Fortune." A brief account of its coming seems vital to the more sustained work which was destined to follow it. I was not present at the next regular meeting of the society; but at its close I was summoned to the telephone and informed that Mark Twain had come again and had said that "the Hannibal girl" was the one for whom he and Mrs. Hays had been waiting. When they asked him what he meant, the planchette made reply:

"Consult your record for 1911."

One of the early volumes of the society's record was brought forth, and a curious fact that all the members of the society had forgotten was unearthed. About a year after his passing out, Mr. Clemens had told Mrs. Hays that he had carried with him much valuable literary material which he yearned to send back, and that he would transmit stories through her, if she could find just the right person to sit with her at the transmission board. Although she experimented with each member of the club, and with several of her friends who were sympathetic though not avowed investigators, he was not satisfied with any of them. Then she gave up the attempt and dismissed it from her mind. A twenty-minute test with me seemed to convince him that in me he had found the negative side of the mysterious human mechanism for which he had been waiting.

The work of transmitting that first story was attended with the greatest difficulty. No less than three distinct styles of diction, accompanied by correspondingly distinct motion in the planchette under our fingers, were thrust into the record. At first we were at a loss to understand these intrusions. That they were intrusions there could be no doubt. In each case there was a sharp deviation from the plot of the story, as it had been given to us in the synopsis. After one of these experiences, which resulted in the introduction of a paragraph that was rather clever but not at all pertinent, Mark regained control with the impatiently traced words:

"Every scribe here wants a pencil on earth."

Not until the middle of summer did we achieve that sureness of touch which now enables us to recognize, intuitively, the presence of the one scribe whose thoughts we are eager to transmit. That the story of Jap Herron and the two short stories which preceded it are the actual post-mortem work of Samuel L. Clemens, known to the world as Mark Twain, we do not for one moment doubt. His individuality has been revealed to us in ways which could leave no question in our minds. The little, intimate touches which reveal personality are really of more importance than the larger and more conspicuous fact that neither Mrs. Hays nor I could have written the fiction that has come across our transmission board. Our literary output is well known, and not even the severest psychological skeptic could assert that it bears any resemblance to the literary style of "Jap Herron."

Mrs. Hays has found the best market for her short stories with one of the large religious publishing houses, and in the early days Mark Twain seemed to fear that her subconscious mind might inadvertently color or distort his thought, in process of transmission. We had come to the end of our fourth session when he added this:

"There will be minor errors that you will be able to take care of. I don't object. Only—don't try to correct my grammar. I know what I want to say. And, dear ladies, when I say d-a-m-n, please don't write d-a-r-n. Don't try to smooth it out. This is not a smooth story."

For most of the remainder of the excerpt, Hutchings goes on to prove (or rather, defend?) the authenticity of the laborious task of dictating this novel from beyond the grave. There are numerous humorous "quotes" from the ghost of Samuel Clemens as well as a nicely detailed description of the board itself:

The board, on which two short stories and a novel have already been transmitted, is one of the ordinary varieties, a polished surface over which the planchette glides to indicate the letters of the alphabet and the figures from 1 to 10. In the main our dictation came without any apparent need for marks of punctuation. Occasionally the words "quotation marks," or "Put that in quotes" would be interjected. Once when my intonation, as I pronounced the words for the amanuensis who was keeping our record, seemed to indicate a direct statement, the planchette whirled under our fingers and traced the crisp statement, "I meant that for a question."

When I told my husband of these grippingly intimate evidences of an unseen personality, it occurred to him that a complete set of punctuation marks, carefully applied in India ink, where the pointer of the planchette could pick them out as they were required, would facilitate the transmission of sustained narrative. To him it seemed that the absence of these marks on the board must be maddening, especially to Mark Twain, whose thought could be hopelessly distorted by the omission of so trivial a thing as a comma, and whose subtle use of the colon was known to all the clan of printers. Before our next meeting the board had been duly adorned with ten of the most important marks, including the hyphen and the M-dash. The comma was at the head of the right-hand column and the apostrophe at the bottom. My husband, Mrs. Hays, and I knew exactly what all these markings meant, yet we had some confusion because Mark insisted on using the comma when he wished to indicate a possessive case. The sentence was this, as I understood it:

"I was not wont to disobey my father, scommand."

Instantly my husband, who had become interested and had taken the place of our first amanuensis, perceived that I had made a mistake, when I pronounced the combination, "f-a-t-h-e-r, comma, s-c-o-m-m-a-n-d."

"But," I defended myself, "the pointer went to the comma. I can see now that it should have been the apostrophe." As I spoke the pointer of the planchette traced the words on the board:

"Edwin did a pretty piece of work, but that apostrophe is too far down. I am in danger of falling off the board every time I make a run for it."

Hutchings made numerous attempts to prove that her work was legitimate and that the ghost of Twain asked for her specifically. (Methinks the lady doth protest too much.) Her insistence that no one among them had read Twain's memoirs conflicts with the clear knowledge of his style when she says, "Then the outline of a typical Mark Twain story came in short, explosive sentences." It is also important to remember that at the time, Hutchings had minor work as a journalist but was otherwise considered a housewife of Missouri, and her writings were dismissed as musings or "little hobbies" by her family and other professorial types. Of course, she also had a friend in the channeling business . . .

If the name Emily Grant Hutchings rings a bell, it could be because of the more well-known automatic writing and channeled materials of Patience Worth. Patience Worth was the name of a spirit contacted by one Pearl Lenore Curran (1883–1937)—a St. Louis housewife with a literary penchant—who produced several novels as well as volumes of poetry and prose that Pearl claimed had been channeled to her by Patience. As it so happens, Emily Grant Hutchings and Pearl Lenore Curran were friends, and in 1912, Hutchings brought a Ouija board over to Curran's house and the two began to dabble in their own version of the psychic arts.

Curran made contact with the spirit of Patience Worth and was compelled to spend endless hours communicating and transcribing her works. In 1917 Hutchings published the previously discussed "lost novel of Mark Twain" *Jap Herron*. By that time "Patience" had become quite the buzz. By 1917 five of Patience's poems were noted as some of the finest poetry published that year, and by 1918 the *New York Times* was calling her first novel a "feat of literary composition." (And it stands to reason that Hutchings was encouraged by the early success of her friend's channeled work and endeavored to achieve the same.)

Did Pearl actually channel the works of a long-dead woman, a woman from the late 1600s who lived "across the sea" somewhere in England and came to the United States, where she met her untimely death by "Indians"? Based on the details that Curran provided, it seemed that Patience would have lived in Dorset, but no record of a woman by that name ever existed, nor are there records of such a woman immigrating to the St. Louis area.

As any writer can attest, some of the descriptions that Pearl gave of the manner in which the stories "came to her" from beyond the Ouija board sound not unlike the way any artist might describe their muse. There is, undoubtedly, something of a trance that takes place when the creativity begins to flow. For a woman in the early twentieth century, at a time when the Spiritualist movement was gaining in popularity—a woman who perhaps did not have the courage or means to declare herself "a writer"—the spirit-board and psychic arts were a means to being heard and not immediately dismissed as another simple housewife hobbyist.

Regardless of whether you believe that Patience Worth was a pen name or a spirit, there's no denying that Curran went on to become an accomplished and impressive writer under this name, and she garnered much publicity. She was repeatedly the subject of discussion among Spiritualist groups, believers and skeptics alike. In 1916, Casper Yost published an entire work, *Patience Worth: A Psychic Mystery*, examining the work and her methods for both fraud and genuine psychic phenomena. (He ended up without any conclusive statements on either side.) In 1927 Walter Franklin Prince dedicated 509 pages to his cross-examination of the subject in *The Case of Patience Worth*. This work was published by the Boston Society for Psychical Research, a group known for debunking hoaxes and charlatans of the psychic arts—of which there were many. To this day, there are just as many believers on both sides.

The Society for Psychical Research was no stranger to extensive investigation of female mediums. Mrs. Leonora Piper (1857–1950) was under their watchful eye for an examination that lasted fifteen years (!!) that, ultimately, concluded no evidence of false trance or hoax. The story of Leonora Piper is a truly remarkable one.

Piper came to her powers after being diagnosed with a tumor. Not only was she vetted by the Society for Psychical Research, but also one Dr. Hodgson (who called Madame Blavatsky and the Theosophical Society charlatans) agreed that Mrs. Piper was the real deal. Piper "hosted" more than one entity, including a French doctor name Phinuit, an actress called Mrs. Siddons, Johann Sebastian Bach, Henry Wadsworth Longfellow, Commodore Vanderbilt (the Italian multimillionaire), and a young Italian girl named Loretta Ponchini. By some accounts she also channeled Abraham Lincoln and George Washington! Dr. Phinuit is said to be her primary "control" and appeared most regularly and readily, speaking in a unique French dialect.

Although she is largely unknown today, Mrs. Piper became one of the most talked about mediums of her time. As the story goes, she was suffering from a brain tumor and went to see a well-known Spiritualist and psychic medium, after which she began to exhibit signs of her own mediumship. She became the subject of extensive investigation by numerous paranormal societies as well as scientists and professors. One of the most notable was William James of Harvard University. The original French translations of Phinuit's conversations were done by Minot Savage, a then member of the Society for Psychical Research. In 1904, with the help of Savage's translations, Noralie Robertson published *Mrs. Piper and the Society for Psychical Research*, which explores both the story of how Piper came to channel as well as her resilience against examination after examination, concluding that after fifteen years of experimenting and investigating Mrs. Piper, no evidence of fraud was found. Robertson writes (on behalf of the Society):

> Mrs. Piper's mediumship is one of the most
> perfect which has ever been discovered. In
> any case, it is the one which has been the most
> perseveringly, lengthily and carefully studied
> by highly competent men. Members of the
> Society for Psychical Research have studied the
> phenomena presented by Mrs. Piper during
> fifteen consecutive years. They have taken all
> the precautions necessitated by the strange-
> ness of the case, the circumstances, and the
> surrounding scepticism; they have faced and

minutely weighed all hypotheses. In future the most orthodox psychologists will be unable to ignore these phenomena when constructing their systems; they will be compelled to examine them and find an explanation for them, which their preconceived ideas will sometimes render it difficult to do.

In spite of the findings of the exhaustive research by the society, many people at the time and to this day are sure that Piper was not a master medium but rather a master of trickery. She faired so well under examination because she could read the subtlest of notions in others: muscle movement and facial twitching. There were accounts of attending séances hosted by Mrs. Piper in which nothing was, in fact, correct or channeled accurately. The maids gossiped that she got her "facts" directly from books and conversations with family members, or that she even paid household servants to divulge secrets before a prominent family came for a reading. Several mentalists and magicians at the time reported deliberately tricking Piper into providing false info. Nonetheless, she remained a prosperous and popular medium in her day and was continually consulted on matters of great importance to prominent families, despite the publicized shortcomings of her abilities. She remained rather flush (in 1910 a session with her cost around $20) and was hostess to séances and psychic salons that ranged from traditional to automatic writing and beyond. The sensationalism that she caused no doubt encouraged both Emily Grant Hutchings and Pearl Curran and vice versa. It was a fine time to be a psychic woman.

Sex before Duty

When it comes to channeled material, few stories compare to that of Ida C. Craddock (1857–1902). Unlike Mrs. Piper, Pearl Curran, and Mrs. Hutchings, Craddock was not widely known for her channeled works. She was a nineteenth-century advocate of free speech and women's rights at a time when both were not only unpopular but punishable by law. Craddock was persecuted by Anthony Comstock and the Suppression for Moral Vice for distributing "lewd materials" via the U.S. Postal Service. Craddock published and sent out pamphlets to young married couples and would-be brides with information about what to expect on the wedding night—a topic that was not at all discussed and left many a young bride terrified. Comstock eventually successfully arrested and tried her under the Comstock Law, but rather than face life in prison or life in an institution, Craddock ended her own life. Somewhat lesser known is that Ida claimed to never have had sexual relations with a man, but that all of her "wedding night" knowledge came directly from her intercourse with Soph, an angelic being. Craddock's *Psychic Wedlock* was held with great regard (and is still) in many magical circles. Even Aleister Crowley revered her. He said her work *Heavenly Bridegrooms* "is one of the most remarkable human documents ever produced." While many purport that Craddock did, in fact, have human lovers (illicit and multiple), she remains one of the most essential, if unsung, heroes of women's rights and spiritual and sexual freedom. Read Vere Chappell's remarkable *Sexual Outlaw, Erotic Mystic: The Essential Ida Craddock* to find out more about her life's work along with details of her magical and moral contributions throughout her short life.

> **Even Aleister Crowley revered her.**

A Rose by Any Other Name

This next story comes from Bo Luellen, a veteran ghost and paranormal investigator and host of the infamous podcast *Paranormal Odyssey*. His first paranormal encounter came when he was just sixteen, when he discovered an unexplained horse mutilation. In 1999 he joined a paranormal investigation team based in Oklahoma and spent more than seven years investigating cryptids, ghosts, and UFOs throughout the region. He currently lives in Oklahoma, where he continues to seek out things that go bump in the night. One evening, he told me this story about a ghost investigation with a surprise ending.

The Rose Case

It was the summer of 2006, and I was running a paranormal research and investigation team in Tulsa, Oklahoma. I had been working cases every weekend since 1999 and had some experience under my belt. My team consisted of friends, work colleagues, and members of prior para-research teams I had been part of. A coworker—Tracy, age thirty-two—approached me stating that her elderly parents' house had been haunted by their Aunt Rose for over twenty years. She wanted our team to come out to investigate and see if we could get evidence of the phenomenon. The following is my account of the details of that investigation to the best of my ability. I've changed the names to protect the privacy of those involved.

> **They told our interviewers of black shadows that would fly along the walls and would occasionally communicate with them.**

First, we sent interviewers to the house to take statements. The home was owned by Gerald and Evelynn Carter, both in their late sixties. They told our interviewers of black shadows that would fly along the walls and would occasionally communicate with them. The house was built in the mid 1960s, and had a sizable backyard. After a few hours of assessing the homeowners and recording their story, our team scheduled the investigation.

The next weekend our team arrived to investigate using EVP recorders, EMF meters, laser thermometers, and camcorders. We worked efficiently: we interviewed neighbors; we had the homeowners retell their story to note any inconsistencies; and we sent a sweep team in to take photos before the techs set up. It was a "by the book" case and each member of our investigative team knew their role.

During the investigation we requested that the family stay outside of the house to avoid getting false EVP artifacts. Gerald and Evelynn agreed, and were joined by their daughter (Tracy) and her husband. I honestly believe they thought it was going to be like one of the ghost hunter shows so popular on TV at that time. After two hours we packed up our equipment and told the clients we would analyze the data and then get back to them. They were grateful but disappointed that we didn't see anything. They seemed adamant that something was haunting the house.

That's when a technician, Sean, spoke up. Sean was a good investigator and showed some aptitude toward psychic ability. I regularly gave him a Zener Test (Rhind Test), which uses statistical probability to eliminate chance from a series of test questions in order to qualify an individual as having a sixth sense. Sean always scored unusually high on this test, and I had learned to give him some latitude when dealing with clients.

Without any prior knowledge of Tracy's background, Sean said to her (in full view of the entire team and the family), "When you were thirteen or fourteen years old, you used a Ouija board in this house. It wasn't your board, was it?"

We all froze in place, as Sean was either going way out on a limb with a hunch or was tapping into something else. Tracy's eyes welled up with tears, and she covered her mouth. It took her a moment to collect herself. She replied, "Yes. I was fourteen years old and a friend brought one over. We were having a slumber party, and it was a fun thing to do."

This caused a stir in her family. Oklahoma is part of the Bible Belt, and Tracy's mother Evelynn immediately began to chastise her in front of everyone, as the use of the Ouija board was considered witchcraft and a sin according to their Pentecostal religion. It took several minutes to get everyone calm again.

Sean continued, "What did the board tell you?"

Tracy looked at her husband and said, "It gave me his name." She was referring to her husband, Sean. "We asked it who I would marry, and the board spelled out a first name." The small family and part of the team went into a uproar. People were crying from sheer fright. Evelynn, a slight woman, went from conservative to aggressive. She grabbed her daughter's arm, and the two began to yell at one another. It was a surreal moment for everyone. Here we were in a suburban neighborhood, watching a devoutly religious family melt down as they realized their lives had been influenced by some unknown force for decades.

Once they'd settled down, Sean stated, "You opened a vortex that day, and something stepped through. That something wasn't your Aunt Rose. It has been here ever since. I can't tell you its intentions, and it could be harmless."

Once again the family became unruly. I told our team to pack up and informed the clients we would return with a data analysis. Getting packed up was tense. Sean was being peppered with questions by the family, and I became afraid that

> **"You opened a vortex that day, and something stepped through."**

they might find some way to blame him. We regrouped at a coffee shop, where we all went over our data on the spot. Nothing came up on any video, the EVPs were clean, and we only had one artifact in one picture. As standard procedure, I developed a PowerPoint with the results of the data to present to the client. I decided to include the photo with the artifact, which we thought was most assuredly a camera strap caught by the flash. I usually try to include pictures like this to give the client a sense of how easily an untrained researcher can be fooled by a piece of false evidence.

When I returned to work the next Monday, Tracy was completely closed off. She did not want to discuss the investigation under any circumstances. She stated that the family "discussion" (which sounded more like a fight to me) had continued all weekend. Her mother was upset that Tracy had never disclosed her "practicing witchcraft." A small family feud had developed in our absence, and even more family members had been brought into the mix.

After two weeks I returned to the clients' house with my lead investigator to reveal our evidence to them. Not surprisingly, the mood was tense from the moment we stepped foot back into the house. This time only Gerald and Evelynn were present. After some pleasantries, we set up in the kitchen and began the PowerPoint presentation of our findings: slide after slide showing no evidence. The last slide was the photo with the "camera strap" artifact in frame. As soon as it came up in the slides, Gerald said, "There is your boyfriend."

My lead investigator and I stared at each other wide-eyed. "What do you mean?" I asked him.

Evelynn pursed her lips tight together like she had just eaten a lemon as Gerald continued, "It's that thing! She loves it! She spends more time talking to *it* than she does to me!"

The old woman responded, "Well, at least it listens to me!"

The two began to argue over one another, and at one point I thought they were going to get physical. During the heated cussing match from these two elderly Pentecostal mega-Christians, my lead and I heard them talk about some shocking details. The woman admitted to having not slept with her husband for twenty years and said that the entity had been "giving her all she needed." The man stated that he couldn't even sleep in the same bed with his wife or *it* would become angry. After several minutes of this, my teammate and I left, showing ourselves to the door. The drive back to our rally point was like a roller-coaster ride, with a bunch of shouts of "Can you believe that?!" and several "Oh my God, that woman is having sex with an entity!"

We never went back to that family and were never called back. We logged the case, and continued our adventures.

Belly Teller

Gastromancy, or divination from the belly, is now generally explained by ventriloquism, the voice in both cases sounding low and hollow, as if issuing from the ground . . . another method of practicing the ancient *gastromancy* connects it with crystal-seeing, as vessels of round glass, and full of clear water, were used, which were placed before several lighted candles. In this case, a young boy or girl was generally the seer, and the demon was summoned in a low voice by the magician. Replies were then obtained from the magical appearances seen in the illuminated glass vessels.

—LEWIS SPENCE, *AN ENCYCLOPEDIA OF OCCULTISM*

Queen Hélène

Hélène Smith (1861–1929) started out life as commonly as any of us—or at least as commonly as any child born into a middle-class family in 1860s France. She was said to be a dreamy child but still rather robust, and according to Beckles Willson in his book *Occultism and Common-*

Sense, "from the age of fifteen she [had been] employed in a large commercial establishment in Geneva, and [held] a position of some responsibility." Perfectly nice, normal girl, right? Things changed dramatically when, in 1892, the then-thirtysomething Hélène was invited to attend a Spiritualist circle. It became immediately apparent that she was a powerful medium. She had visions and heard voices. She assisted in table tipping—a common practice in séances where the participants would attempt to levitate or move the table. And then. Oh then. Something within Smith was unleashed. It didn't take long until her abilities made table tipping and spirit-boards seem like mere child's play. Smith began experiencing trancelike states in which she channeled spirits such as Victor Hugo, Marie Antoinette, and Mirabeau, Prince of Orleans. She actually gained the reputation for being the "muse of automatic writing." But in 1894 she stunned the attendants in her circle by claiming that she was able to go off-planet. Willson writes:

> **It didn't take long until her abilities made table tipping and spirit-boards seem like mere child's play.**

In November 1894, the spirit of the entranced medium was wafted—not without threatenings of sea-sickness—through the cosmic void, to arrive eventually on the planet Mars. Thereafter night after night she described to the listening circle the people of our neighbouring planet, their food, dress, and ways of life. At times she drew pictures of the inhabitants, human and animal—of their houses, bridges, and other edifices, and of the surrounding landscape. Later she both spoke and wrote freely in the Martian language. From the writings reproduced in M. Flournoy's book it is clear that the characters of the Martian script are unlike any in use on earth, and that the words (of which a translation is furnished) bear no resemblance, superficially at least, to any known tongue. The spirits—for several dwellers upon Mars used Hélène's organism to speak and write through—delivered themselves with freedom and fluency, and were consistent in their usage both of the spoken and the written words. In fact, Martian, as used by the entranced Hélène, has many of the characteristics of a genuine language; and it is not surprising that some of the onlookers, who may have hesitated over the authenticity of the other revelations, were apparently convinced that these Martian utterances were beyond the common order of nature.

While many were skeptical of Hélène's actual abilities, one woman believed. A well-to-do American Spiritualist known only as Mrs. Jackson, became her patron. Smith accepted Jackson's offer and lived out much of her life dedicating herself to the pursuit of the psychic arts through séances and trance-mediumship as well as painting her visions.

The Fantastic Fox Sisters

Spiritualism, the belief that the spirits of the dead not only have the ability to communicate with the living but also the desire to do so reached its peak in the United States between the 1840s and the 1920s. In 1897 there were close to eight million subscribers to this belief throughout the United States and Europe, thanks in no small part to three sisters from New York, Leah (1831–

1890), Margaret (1833–1893), and Kate (1837–1892) Fox. Margaret and Kate both convinced their sister that they were receiving messages from the dead using "rappings" (the tapping out of messages on a table, board, etc. to communicate from the afterlife).

The eldest sister, Leah, managed the newfound careers of her younger sisters, making them some of the most famous mediums of their time. The celebrity psychic life proved too much for Kate and Margaret especially, and they were both rumored to be heavy drinkers. Their world began to crumble when, in 1851, a relative of theirs claimed publically that she had assisted in a séance and the rappings were a hoax. The claims were not enough to ruin the careers of the legendary sisters, however, and they continued making money as mediums for a number of years.

But by 1888 the sisters were in quite a state: Kate's husband had passed away, and her drinking was out of control. Leah staged an intervention of sorts and implored Kate to remand care of the two children over to her elder sister, as Leah did not think Kate was fit to look after them. Angry that Leah was trying to take her children, Kate accepted an offer from a reporter for $1,500 if she would admit in print and in public that the rappings were fake. Meanwhile, Margaret had repented, was returning to the Catholic faith, and believed that the confession would help alleviate the guilt she felt. And so, in 1888, they signed a statement admitting the hoax and even demonstrating their method. This brought (of course) an end to their psychic careers. The money soon dried up, and all three sisters died penniless within a five-year period.

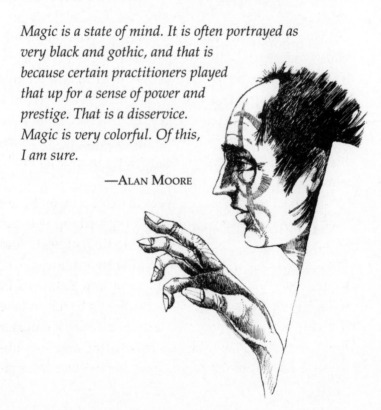

Magic is a state of mind. It is often portrayed as very black and gothic, and that is because certain practitioners played that up for a sense of power and prestige. That is a disservice. Magic is very colorful. Of this, I am sure.

—ALAN MOORE

Over Hill and Over Lily Dale

Many sites around the world lay claim to being meccas for Spiritualists and psychics (Santa Fe, Denver, San Francisco . . .), but there's one superstar that is more than a magnet for freaks and freethinkers: the town of Lily Dale in New York was founded on this premise. Incorporated in 1879 as a meeting place for Spiritualists, its name changed to The City of Light and then again to Lily Dale Assembly (in 1906), although it is mostly called Lily Dale today. With a small population of less than 300 year-round residents, it maintains its almost 140-year tradition as a center for psychic arts, communing with the dead, and séances. You'll find classes in mediumship and famous lecturers including Deepak Chopra, John Edwards, and James Van Praagh. You'll find a museum dedicated to the history of Spiritualism, new age stores, and plenty of ready psychics and healers on hand.

Try to Keep an Open Mind

Amy and Isaac Post were a pretty radical couple for the 1840s. As outspoken abolitionists, it isn't surprising that their open-minded attitude meant that not only were they Quakers, freethinkers, and women's rights advocates, they were also believers in the Spiritualist movement. Not only did they hold regular abolitionist meetings in their home, where they hosted Susan B. Anthony and Frederick Douglass as lecturers, they became close personal friends with Douglass and helped him establish his legendary newspaper *The North Star*. The Post home was a station along the Underground Railroad, and it is said that they housed more than twenty escaped slaves.

Amy Post was extremely outspoken in the women's movement. She was friends with Harriet Ann Jacobs, who wrote *Incidents in the Life of a Slave Girl*. But in the company of radicals and freethinkers, they also invited the Fox Sisters into their home. Kate and Margaret Fox were just at the beginning of their career as infamous mediums, and the Posts were introduced to a new world of psychics, séances, and the Spiritualist belief in afterlife communication. In fact, Isaac Post became a medium that channeled the ghosts of Benjamin Franklin and other notables in the book *Voices from the Spirit World* (published in 1852).

Is That an EVP, or Are You Just Happy to See Me?

Ron Kolek is the founder and lead investigator of The New England Ghost Project. With a degree in environmental science, he was the ultimate skeptic. However, a near-death experience changed all that. No longer blinded by his skepticism, he now uses his scientific background to seek the truth about the paranormal. In addition to hosting *Ghost Chronicles* on Ghostvillage Radio and iTunes, he hosts a weekly internet radio show on Toginet.com, and has cowritten two books with Maureen Wood: *The Ghost Chronicles* and *Ghost a Day.* As I write, Ron has a new book scheduled for publication by Weiser Books in 2018. Ron has been a supporter of mine since *The Book of the Bizarre*, and he didn't hesitate to share his story with me. I only lament, dear readers, that you cannot hear him tell this to you in person.

Ron Kolek's Pot House

I was called in to do an investigation on a property that was in foreclosure. When we arrived, the house was mostly empty: devoid of furniture, except for a couple of items, but the homeowners were still there. Maureen Wood, my partner in investigations (and many other ghostly ventures) and a transmedium, was standing in the middle of the room with a pendulum, making contact with the spirit. I had my EMF meter with me. It wasn't long before the meter started going off. We began walking around the room and the house. At times the meter was silent, and other times it was lit up and making noises. It had the feeling of something playful, almost like a game of hide-and-seek. As we continued to walk around, I began to recognize that I was following something. The EMF reader would go off, and I would go in that direction. I would move around the room until it would go off again.

> **It had the feeling of something playful, almost like a game of hide-and-seek.**

Maureen asked the spirits their names and what they wanted. Right away she told me their names were Elizabeth and Michael. Maureen thanked them, and we continued to follow in this manner—Maureen asking questions and making contact, and me following with my EMF reader—tracking the signs of their presence as we went down the stairs and throughout the rest of the house. We continued, by indication of the EMF reader, out of the back of the house and across the backyard into the woods. Of course, at this point it's coming on midnight (as in any good ghost story), and we proceeded into the dark forest. It was not long before we came upon a small family graveyard. There were only a few graves surrounded by an old cast-iron fence. It was built up a bit, on a stone edge. We spotted a gate in the fence and headed inside the cemetery. With less than a dozen graves, we walked carefully by each one. When we came to two small headstones, the EMF reader started going off like crazy. Maureen told

me that these must be their graves, the children, Elizabeth and Michael. After that the meter went dead. So we headed back to the house to close up the investigation and head home. We gave these two names and the location of the house to our research department, and it actually turned out that the names Elizabeth and Michael were, in fact, those of two children who had lived there and died.

But that's not all.

At the end of the night, the homeowner was telling us about her bad luck. And she also mentioned that when she moved into the house she had noticed that there were little coins along the windowsill, all facedown. She had collected them and shortly thereafter began to experience paranormal activity. Her luck went from bad to worse, and soon her house was in foreclosure. We continued talking with her, asking if she'd ever had any other paranormal experiences. Eventually, she admitted to us that she used to do the Ouija board alone in the house. In fact, she told us she used to smoke pot and do the Ouija board, alone in the house. Once she'd confessed this, she really began to open up and admitted that she had made contact with a spirit who became her friend. It became a regular thing, and one time she smoked pot and invited the spirit to channel into her body. She kept describing "him" as her friend. "He always tells me about the good sales at Macy's," she told us.

We finished our investigation and left the house. It took me some time, but I did eventually find an example of coins being placed facedown on a windowsill, so that when the Devil sends his minions to go into the house they would look down and grow confused by the coins. I wrote about this story in my book *Ghost Chronicles*.

It's called "The House That Went to Pot."

—RON KOLEK, AS TOLD TO VARLA VENTURA

A Woman's Intuition

The wife of Ulysses S. Grant woke up on April 14, 1865, with a terrible, foreboding feeling. She insisted that she and her husband leave Washington, DC at once, though it meant standing up President Lincoln's invitation to the theater that evening. She begged her husband that they leave town, and he acquiesced. That same day, at the theater, Lincoln was shot and killed by John Wilkes Booth. Booth's papers later revealed that Grant, too, was on his hit list.

The True Story of Startling Séances in San Francisco

Published in 1900, *The True Story of Startling Séances in San Francisco* is an account of a series of séances that took place in the year 1893. It would not be so unusual to think of such a concept, as séances and paranormal parlor games were at the height of their popularity. But what makes this collection unique is the players involved: William Randolph Hearst, for example; the district attorney Captain W. S. Barnes; and even the mayor of the city himself. Mayor Levi Richard Ellert (1857–1901) reigned over San Francisco during the tender years of 1893–1895 and was the first San Francisco mayor to have been born in California. Perhaps his NorCal status is to what we owe his natural openness to the Other Side.

The author inserts himself in the 1900 story as chief witness and recorder, yet never reveals his true identity. However, parts of what became the book were originally published in an 1898 article in the *Sacramento Daily Union*—some five years after the fact. While the author was in the offices of Senator J. D. Spencer in Modesto, California, they were approached by a well-known medium at the time, Dr. Louis Schlesinger. Our author and the good senator became quite convinced of

Schlesinger's abilities. Reportedly, the medium walked into the offices and said:

> "Gentlemen, I am Dr. Louis Schlesinger, the famous Spiritualist medium. It is well known that I can talk with the good angels, and I desire to have a series of séances here in Modesto."

After being convinced that Schlesinger was the real deal, the senator, Schlesinger, and our mystery man proceed north to convince the good mayor of San Francisco to conduct a séance in his own office.

> With the memory of my Modesto experiences fresh in mind, I decided, when I came upon Dr. Schlesinger in San Francisco, in 1893, to institute a series of daylight séances in the presence of some of the most distinguished citizens of San Francisco. As I was then a writer of the San Francisco *Daily Examiner* staff I found rare opportunities for enlisting the men desired in the experiments. I was not then, nor am I now, in any manner affiliated with Spiritualists, nor do I set forth the facts of this narrative for the purpose of making converts to any theory of mind or matter.

The manuscript from which this work is printed was written at the time of the matters recorded, on an order from the *Examiner*. Owing to the fact that Mayor Ellert afterwards regretted that he had allowed a séance to be held in his office, the *Examiner* was induced to suppress the story, which now appears in detail for the first time. It should be borne in mind that all that follows was written at the events described.

Later, our anonymous author details his interaction with the local paper to publish the story. He claims that he had visited the offices of William Randolph Hearst and pitched the idea as an intriguing series.

Ambitious to arrange something of unusual interest, I approached Mr. Hearst and S. S. Chamberlain, who were in charge of the news department of the paper. I told them what I had seen Dr. Schlesinger do in Modesto, and outlined the plans that were afterwards carried out—séances at the office of Mayor Ellert and the Chief of Police, in the presence of prominent citizens. First, however, it was necessary for the editors to see the medium at their offices; for they feared there would be some failure, and that the citizens invited would be disgusted because of their loss of time in useless experiments.

For these reasons, therefore, the first sittings were at the editorial offices of the *Examiner*, where the editors were as much puzzled as anybody else. They were at once convinced that, however he performed his feats, Dr. Schlesinger was at least not a bungling master of the black art. Several intelligent observers were present, among them one or two of the brightest newspapermen in the city. The experiments were not only carefully noted, but they were viewed with grave suspicion. They were, however, wholly informal and merely preliminary to the more important and prolonged séances that followed at the office of the Mayor of the city, and later at the office of and in the presence of the city's Chief of Police. A few facts concerning the occurrences at the *Examiner* office are given that the reader may have the full benefit of the story.

One of the investigators (Managing Editor A. B. Henderson) wrote a number of names on slips of paper, before Dr. Schlesinger arrived. They were not seen or known to any one save the person that prepared them, and the slips on which they were written were carefully folded and clasped in a bundle, by a rubber band or elastic. Great pains were taken by Mr. Henderson to prevent the medium from handling or seeing the slips. Without seeing the writing, Dr. Schlesinger at once gave the names correctly. One of them was that of Thaddeus Stevens, the eminent Pennsylvanian; and when the folded slip on which his name was written was touched by Mr. Henderson, the medium said: "That is the name of Thaddeus Stevens, who knew you well. He calls you Alexander, and sends you his love."

Then the name of the sitter's deceased uncle was properly announced, though it had not been written on any of the slips. Correct information was also given concerning the uncle's religion while "in the flesh."

S. S. Chamberlain, now Managing Editor of the Philadelphia *North American*, (then News Editor of the *Examiner*) was one of the investigators. He wrote down, on separate slips of paper, the names of many living and dead persons, but, contrary to the medium's request, he did not write the names of persons he had ever known. In a few moments Dr. Schlesinger read the names correctly while the slips were beyond his reach, and firmly clasped in Chamberlain's hand. They were of such persons as John Ruskin, Ralph Waldo Emerson, Shakespeare, Longfellow, etc.

Our author, perhaps a bit miffed by the cancellation of the publication as promised, continues again to mention that he was encouraged to write the accounts but was rejected by the editor "for personal reasons."

A faithful report of all that occurred was submitted to the managing editor of the paper, who at once decided that a series of similar experiments, conducted at the office of the Mayor of the city and others, in broad daylight, would make the basis for some interesting Sunday specials. Under his instructions I arranged the seances, and was present at all of them. I subsequently wrote a faithful account of what occurred, but the articles were rejected by the editor of the Sunday *Examiner* for personal reasons. This volume embraces the substance of what was then prepared.

His first order of business in his 1898 article, naturally in response to being repressed, is to publish the names of all of those present:

> Mayor L. R. Ellert; Chief of Police Crowley; Judge Robert Ferral; District Attorney W. S. Barnes; President Theodore F. Bonnet of the Press Club; Grant Carpenter, exPresident of the Press Club; Dr. R. E. Bunker, also Charles L. Patton, Republican Central Committeeman; H. H. McCloskey of Merced, and others.

But what took place during these séances? Were there more parlor tricks? It appears Dr. Schlesinger's favorite tactic was the slips-of-paper method. In the article as well as in the later lengthier publication, our anonymous reporter cites sworn statements by the DA and the judges, among others. The first séance took place in the daylight hours at the office of the mayor (does he point out the daylight hours to make it clear that these parlor games were on the people's dime?) when

> the experiments with Mayor L. R. Ellert, who sprang from his chair and positively declined

to be thrown into a trance condition when the doctor requested him thus to visit the spirit world, were fully as startling as those with Chief Crowley.

The next daylight séance was held in the office of Chief of Police Crowley. Here is the account:

The Doctor's favorite method of communicating startling information was to have the sitters write, before they came into his presence, fifteen or twenty names of living and dead friends. Each name being on a separate piece of paper, the visitors were requested to fold each slip tightly, so as to preclude any possibility of its being read by the medium. This done, the slips, all of equal size, were put into a hat and thoroughly shuffled. The Doctor would then say: "Pick out any slip yourself, and I will read it without looking and before you yourself know what the name is." There would then be raps, and in a few seconds the Doctor would give the name correctly. These names were written and folded in a room apart from the Doctor.

"Granting that there is such a thing as mind-reading," said Chief Crowley, "I do not think mind-reading would account for what was done for me, because he read things that were not in my mind, telling me my mother's maiden name and where she died."

Dr. Schlesinger calls his gift clairaudient mediumship, and says his right ear is deaf to all terrestrial sounds, but quickened, as with a sixth sense, for communications from the other world. He says he can both see and hear spirits, and that bands of them encircle him, and at times, in the presence of some peculiarly "fit" visitors, manifest themselves with great clearness and power. To prove that the sounds he hears are celestial voices, he does many things which baffle those who witness the strange phenomena which abound in his presence wherever he goes.

It was with much difficulty that those who participated in these seances and whose accounts of what they saw are subjoined, were induced to give the medium a hearing. Chief Crowley was particularly opposed to giving serious attention to what he denounced as "trickery and sleight of hand," and afterwards called "marvelous and beyond power of explanation." Finally he wrote down a number of names on separate slips, as explained in the foregoing, and among those names appeared that of his mother—her maiden name. The medium at once told the Chief which pellet contained his mother's name, then read it, and in a few moments told where she died and where she was buried.

A few minutes later the aged Doctor said: "The spirit of Detective Hutton, who died a violent death, hovers near you."

The medium then spoke of matters that were known to nobody but Chief Crowley and the dead detective. This greatly puzzled the Chief, who was later deeply affected over purported messages from a son and others who had been dear to him in life.

Speaking of the purported message from his dead mother the Chief said: "I cannot explain this, which is marvelous, for I do not believe a human being in San Francisco knew that my mother's maiden name was Elizabeth McCarthy, that she died in New Jersey and was buried in New York."

Chief Crowley then wrote down a list of years, among them the year of his mother's death. Dr. Schlesinger pointed to the year 1833 as that of her death.

"Correct!" replied Chief Crowley; whereupon the medium said, "and the name of your father, Patrick J. Crowley, is also here, and he comes with your son Lewis, who has not been dead long."

The Chief thought it the most wonderful performance he had ever seen. "He does marvelous and inexplicable things," said the Chief, "and I'll admit I cannot tell how it is done. While I cannot believe he converses with spirits, I am puzzled. I want to see him again and look into the matter further."

Were these séances actual occurrences, or was the entire scenario invented as a sensational publishing ploy? If he wished to gain fame and fortune, then surely the author would have publicized his own name. Did he seek to destroy the good reputation of these "prominent citizens"? If the answer is yes, then why wait until the mayor is no longer in office, nor the chief of police?

What the eyes see and the ears hear, the mind believes.

—HARRY HOUDINI

Deaf-initely Something

In my family, both of my maternal grandparents were deaf: my grandmother lost her hearing from scarlet fever at the age of ten; my grandfather lost his from spinal meningitis when he was just three years old. They lived in San Francisco and had four children, who were all brought up learning ASL. It was their custom to have little fun sessions of their own. My grandmother would have a few friends over from the Deaf Club, and they'd be laughing and playing cards. They would often all stop and put their hands on the table and actually manage to levitate it. They used to also have my uncle, their eldest son, involved in mentalist games. When he was about nine or ten, their custom was to hide something in the room while the boy was in another room. Then, when he would come in, they would all think about the object and where it was. One of them would then touch my uncle and he would go and find it. This continued occasionally until one time when they did it and he had a seizure and they stopped.

Houdini Approved

Annetta Black, one of the founders of the San Francisco-based Odd Salon—a series of speaker events on weird history, science, and the arts—shared this bit of rather unusual family lore with me:

> My great, great grandfather (allegedly) went to see Houdini late in his career. Got a recommendation to a medium who was purportedly legit. He went, and she sat him down, had him write names of departed loved ones on bits of paper. She then crumpled them up and put them between two slates with a bit of chalk, wrapped them up in a shawl, and laid hands on them. When opened up, the slates were covered in messages to my great, great grandfather including childhood nicknames and little family jokes. The slates still exist and are with my family back east. I have photos!
>
> —ANNETTA BLACK

First Lady of Magic

Annie Fay was the stage name of an Ohio-born medium and mentalist who became well known during the late 1800s during the peak of Spiritualism fever in the United States. Toward the end of her career her psychic powers were proven fraudulent, though as a magician she made history. She used a series of parlor tricks to convince people that they were seeing ghosts and objects move, and that her powers of mentalism could predict the future. It was reputed that she employed assistants to "research" members of the community she would visit on her tours and find out who went to séances and what info was revealed during those sessions. However, unlike Pearl Curran or Emily Hutchings, Annie Fay was a theatrical performer who even made a disclaimer at the beginning of her shows to the effect of "you are welcome to think what you see is real." It is said that she eventually (allegedly) revealed her tricks to Houdini after she retired. Today she is considered one of the pioneers of paranormal and stage mentalism: in 1913 she applied for membership to The Magic Circle, an early magician's alliance that was actually male-only until the 1990s and received the title of "Honorary Lady Associate."

You Might Get Carded

If you don't already worship at the feet of Joe Diamond, you should really get on board. A paranormal magician, he is truly one of a kind. He is an entertainer, mind reader, dream interpreter, radio host and author, and the world record holder for solving the world's largest maze while blindfolded! I am telling you, you need this man in your life. He can find hidden objects in graveyards while blindfolded! There's video proof! When I asked Joe to contribute a story, he told me he had one about a haunted tarot deck, and I was immediately hooked.

The Case of the Haunted Tarot Deck

I have a dear friend, Angel, with whom I stay every time I travel to Florida, which is at least once a year for a regular gig. She is a close friend, and I always look forward to seeing her and her husband.

She has a tarot deck that belongs to her family, but its origins are unknown. It has been around for multiple generations, and her family lore says something about it belonging to an aunt, but no one really knows for sure. Angel has a few decks and reads the tarot, but for whatever reason this particular deck she inherited has always made her feel uneasy.

Before she moved, she decided she would at last just get rid of the deck. She tried, but somehow the deck came back. Numerous times over the years she has tried to get rid of it, even throwing it away, and yet somehow this deck would always reappear.

Naturally, I volunteered to take this odd deck off of her hands. I told her if she really wants rid of it, I'll gladly take it.

So when I arrived for my visit in 2012, she greeted me with the deck. Since I was serious, she said, I should take it now and get it out of her house. I took it out to my car and slipped it into the back passenger seat pocket, where I always keep a notebook or two and a book I'm reading for easy reference. (My friend was in the house during this and did not see where I put this deck.)

We enjoy our visit for the week, and then the time comes for me to leave. I get about two hours' drive down the road when my friend calls and says, "Very funny, Joe." I have no idea what she is talking about, and tell her as much. "The deck, Joe. On the bed. Very funny." I insist I don't know what she means, and then she explains to me that when she went into the room to change the sheets she found the tarot deck there on the bed. Thinking I was pranking her, she called me right away.

I, on the other hand, hadn't thought much about the deck and hadn't touched it since I'd put it in my car that

first day. I told her I was close to a rest stop and would pull over and look in the backseat pocket for the deck. I do, and it is not there. But it gets weirder.

I travel quite a bit, driving six to eight hours for gigs on a regular basis, so I spend a lot of time in my car. Consequently, I clean it out pretty thoroughly every couple of months. And that particular pocket is kind of my go-to where I keep my current notes and whatever I'm reading, so it gets cleaned out frequently.

One year later, in 2013, while making preparations for the same engagement in Florida (and planning to stay with Angel and her family again), I was cleaning my car out readying for the trip. I reached into that backseat pocket, and in it I found one single tarot card. The Knight of Cups.

I immediately called Angel and asked, were all the cards there, and what is the pattern on the back of the cards. She described it and insisted the deck was intact. I asked her to check it again. A few minutes later she called back and said it was, in fact, missing a card: the Knight of Cups. (And add to that, based on my birth sign, this is my signifier card.)

When I finally arrive at her house, she tells me the tarot deck is missing. She can't find it anywhere. We look all over her house and the deck never turns up.

Before I shared this story with you, I called Angel to make sure she was okay with me sharing it, and I implored her to tell me if this was actually an elaborate prank. I told her I would give her kudos for the greatest prank in history. But she insisted she had nothing to do with it. I trust her with my life, and I know she is telling the truth.

While it's possible that the card somehow stayed in the pocket unnoticed, perhaps tucked into a book, and that somehow, after a year of trips and cleaning it went unnoticed (this still doesn't explain how the deck got out of my car back into her house), the odds are really pretty astronomical. In fact, the odds are so astronomical that in my mind they are the equivalent of an astral projecting tarot card!

> **Somehow, the universe dealt me the greatest sleight of hand I've ever seen.**

I used to be a much bigger skeptic, but over the years, experiences like this have made me far less skeptical. Somehow, the universe dealt me the greatest sleight of hand I've ever seen.

—JOE DIAMOND, AS TOLD TO VARLA VENTURA

Tappa, Tappa, Tappa

Back in my apartment in San Francisco, in the final year of my living there, another incident occurred of a tapping/rapping nature. This experience did not in any way affect my decision to leave—if your real estate listing says "haunted" or "near cemetery," I'm more interested than if you told me it has subway tiles and granite countertops. I've seen a few apparitions (and one leprechaun—ask me about that over cocktails sometime), and I've felt things like the sinking weight of some invisible person sitting on the bed. But until this point, I'd never felt such a distinct, physical touch on my own body from a ghost.

> **I woke up to the sensation of a single, strong tap directly to the center of my forehead.**

I woke up to the sensation of a single, strong tap directly to the center of my forehead. The spot on my forehead felt cold, and it was as if a great drop of water had fallen directly onto my head. In fact, I was pretty sure the roof had leaked. When I inspected, there was no water, though my forehead had the lingering chill, as if someone had put a drop of peppermint oil right where the tap had been.

Just then, I heard a gentle laugh from the baby's room as he giggled in his sleep. I crept up to check on him, and he was peacefully asleep. And then just moments later a steady tapping began in the kitchen (down the hall but still relatively close, it's a small apartment). I listened, a little breathless.

Tap tap tap. What was it? The fridge churning? The wind rattling the windows? *Tap tap tap.* Pause. *Tap tap tap.* Pause. This went on for two or three minutes, something that sounded like a cupboard opening and closing. As I made my way cautiously toward the kitchen, the sound stopped. It did not start up again; however, there had been one time years before that I had heard something similar.

That time, I was in the middle of a radio interview (on the topic of the paranormal, of course) and heard the tapping. It lasted about two minutes and then ceased. If it was a ghost, our ghost, it was a gentle one. Honestly, I would have been far more horrified if I had discovered a mighty rodent at work, but as I said, it is rare that I personally had felt the physical presence of anything on my actual body (beyond spine chills and spidey sense), so this incident remains with me today. I can still feel that chilling fingertip-like sensation. But was it a ghost? Or was it simply a dream?

Deep into that darkness peering, long I stood there, wondering, fearing, doubting, dreaming dreams no mortal ever dared to dream before.

—EDGAR ALLAN POE, *THE RAVEN*

Chapter 4

Supernatural Superheroes

*The Secret Lives of Upstanding Citizens Who
Labored Under Cover of Night on Horror
Novels and Other Psychic Pursuits*

Either write something worth reading or do something worth writing.

—BENJAMIN FRANKLIN

Make Mine a Double

In truth, there are very few writers who can say they don't live a double life—and I'm not just referring to pen names. Until you "hit the big time," having a published story or even a book does not afford one enough money to pay the bills, and so writing as a profession—at least for the early years of a serious career—is usually a hobby or something to be achieved while burning the midnight oil. A more laborious day job is needed to make ends meet.

There are writers, and then there are people who write. The following chapter will give you brief snippets and biographical information about some of my

favorite "surprising" citizens, most of whom were alive during the rise of Spiritualism in Victorian England and North America and throughout the infamous "parlor" years of psychic salons and ghost fetish. While many others have made their way into other parts of these books, I wanted to share a few of my favorite and sometimes startling characters who have come to be like close friends on my bookshelf and on these pages.

The Reverend Who Hunted Werewolves

Sabine Baring-Gould was an eclectic man. Born in England in 1834, he is best known for the hymns he composed, among them the widely recognized "Onward, Christian Soldiers." He was married for nearly fifty years and fathered fifteen children. He was a collector of stories and folk songs as well as an accomplished novelist and was known to write while standing. His collection of lore, stories, and philosophies on werewolves, *The Book of Were-wolves*, was published in 1865 and is still one of the largest studies of werewolf lore to this day. He died in 1924 and was buried next to his wife. Throughout his extensive research on everything from medical to psychological to supernatural explanations, Gould seems to conclude that werewolves are most assuredly real. (For more on Gould's work on werewolves, read *Banshees, Werewolves, Vampires and Other Creatures of the Night*.)

The Painter Who Adored Ghosts

Born in England in 1862, Montague Rhodes James (who published as M. R. James) was one of the best ghost-story tellers of his time. Admired by the likes of Lovecraft in his day, he inspired and reshaped the genre of horror fiction, making it more creepily realistic and less fantastical. His works continue to influence modern writers, including Stephen King. M. R. James, for his part, thought that Irish writer Sheridan Le Fanu was the best author of ghost stories at the time (and this is arguably true). In addition to being a gifted storyteller, James was a scholar of medieval works, an art historian, and an accomplished painter. Toward the end of his life he became provost of Eton College. He died in 1936 with many accolades and countless admirers.

If I don't write to empty my mind, I go mad.

—Lord Byron

The Doctor Who Loved Vampires

Horror devotees will recall the story of the infamous gathering at a lake house outside of Geneva, Switzerland, in the summer of 1816, where a small party celebrated the settling darkness by reading ghost stories aloud to one another. Present were the host, Lord Byron, and his guests: Percy Bysshe Shelley, Mary Wollstonecraft (Shelley) and her sister, and Lord Byron's physician—John William Polidori. Polidori was a trained medical doctor, born in England in 1795.

At the prompting of Byron, pens were set to paper to write ghost stories of their own. Here the groundwork was laid for what would become *Mary Shelley's Frankenstein, a Modern Prometheus*. Shelley himself wrote *Fragments of a Ghost Story*, and Byron wrote something called *Fragment of a Novel*. It was Byron's "fragment" that later became the basis for Polidori's *The Vampyre, A Tale*—the first vampire novel published in English, some seventy years before Bram Stoker's *Dracula*. As Byron's personal physician, and a writer and poet in his own right, he traveled throughout Europe at Byron's side.

According to the introduction to *The Vampyre*, sometime after the fated night in Geneva, Polidori approached Byron for permission to spin off of his idea. Byron agreed, as he'd no plans to write further on the idea. When *The Vampyre* was published, it received scathing reviews. Some believed that the work was actually Byron's but he was claiming it Polidori's work to avoid embarrassment, but both Polidori and the other witnesses that night declared it the good doctor's own writing. Polidori died a pauper in London, and evidence suggests that he committed suicide by consuming cyanide.

Thomas Edison's Paranormal Experiments

There are numerous accounts from Edison's personal journals, essays, and letters detailing his attempts to communicate with the dead.

Scientist and legendary inventor Thomas Edison had a bit of a penchant for the paranormal. In the book *The Diary and Sundry Observations of Thomas Alva Edison*, published by the Philosophical Library in 1948, there are numerous accounts from Edison's personal journals, essays, and letters detailing his attempts to communicate with the dead.

The Builder Who Loved Parlor Games

Edward A. Brackett was a noted sculptor and artist of the mid-nineteenth century, possibly most famous for the house he built in Winchester, Massachusetts. The house, which is now a historic site, is composed entirely of octagons. In between his artistic pursuits, family obligations, and business endeavors, Brackett launched a full-scale psychic investigation, which he wrote about and published in a 1908 book called *Materialized Apparitions: If Not Beings from Another Life What Are They?* His story, like so many of the Spiritualist times, has a familiar ring to it. Skeptic starts out with the idea that it's all a fraud, to quickly be astounded and addicted to the process. (It should be noted that most writing about Dr. Coyler suggests that he was not particularly highly regarded in his day—but mesmerism and homeopathy were both thought to be crackpot endeavors.) Brackett writes:

> In 1840 I became acquainted with Dr. Colyer, then lecturing on Mesmerism, at Peel's Museum, New York, and fully believed, at that time, that he was a humbug, and Mesmerism a fraud. Soon after this, while visiting some friends, with Mr. Pendleton, formerly from

Boston, this subject was pretty thoroughly discussed,—Mr. Pendleton insisting that there was truth in it, and that I was not treating it fairly; and he proposed, as a matter of amusement, that I should try the experiment on some one of the party present. Willing to turn the discussion into a less serious form, I consented to take the part assigned me; and soon found, to my astonishment, that I had before me a most excellent clairvoyant subject. What had been started as amusement became a very interesting entertainment, resulting in the meeting of the parties once a week for the purpose of studying Mesmerism.

I have not failed. I've just found 10,000 ways that won't work.

—THOMAS EDISON

The Goblin-Hunting Consulate

It isn't often that a collector of ghostly tales such as myself finds stories that truly make my toes curl. Such was the case with much of the frightening folklore in the 1880 book *British Goblins: Welsh Folk-lore, Fairy Mythology, Legends and Tradition*—some of which I have drawn on for this book, but most assuredly heavily influenced my decision to write my previous book, *Fairies, Pookas, and Changelings*. In spite of the title "British Goblins," this great volume not only includes all manner of terrifying things that scuttle from cupboard to fairy mound, but also has extensive chapters on Pagan holiday and traditional customs, funeral rights, ghosts, and hell-hounds. Its author, William Wirt Sikes (1836–1883), was a writer and journalist appointed to be the U.S. consul at Cardiff, Wales, in 1876. It was there that he undertook the studying and preservation of Welsh folklore and history, and also became acquainted with those things that go bump in the night. Sikes lived in Wales at the end of his life (and died there). I like to picture him sharing a spot of tea with an old grandmother who tells

him a tale from her mother's mother. Or perhaps he is smoking a pipe with an old farmer who has seen with his own eyes some of the creatures who inhabit these pages and knows "for a fact" that the stories are true.

In Sikes's own words, he makes an attempt to classify these creatures from beyond the veil into six main categories:

1. Departed Mortals

2. Goblin Animals

3. Spectres of Natural Objects

4. Grotesque Ghosts

5. Familiar Spirits

6. Death Omens

Séances, haunted houses, an evil tailor, goblins, and wraiths skirted across the desk right alongside declarations of law and order, political paperwork, and invites to soirees. All were creeping about within the life and times of William Wirt Sikes.

The Turn-of-the-Century
Spoken-Word Artist

Ruth McEnery Stuart was an early twentieth-century, American-born writer most known for her contributions to popular publications such as *Harpers Magazine* and *New Princeton Review*. She became most remembered during her writing career (which spanned from 1888 to her death in 1917) for her oral performances of the numerous articles, short stories, and verses she composed. She married just once, to a widowed farmer with eleven children, but after he died she returned to her hometown of New Orleans.

Stuart kept the company of notables of early American literature, including Mark Twain. She was best known for writing dialect, including Creole, Italian, Irish, and African American. In fact, she was one of the few women writing so-called "plantation stories" (published, no less!) at the time and repeatedly had black women as her central characters. That being said, her vernacular is rich with derogatory terms that make a read of many of them more cringe-worthy and frightening than any ghost story she wrote. In fact, her only ghost story was written toward the end of her life. In 1911 she published *The Haunted Photograph* about a poor widow who believes the ghost of her husband appears in an enchanted photograph of him. Her use of colorful dialect in the story pays tribute to her poetic and spoken-word tendencies, making it worthy of a sweet and fast "ghostly" read. There are fun words like "agog" and descriptions of the tawdry woman as a "blondinette typewriter," and quirky expressions like "I'll have to beat my eggs to a fluff even for angel-cake, so's not to have it taste like gingerbread to him."

> *For who can wonder that man should feel a vague belief in tales of disembodied spirits wandering through those places which they once dearly affected, when he himself, scarcely less separated from his old world than they, is for ever lingering upon past emotions and bygone times, and hovering, the ghost of his former self, about the places and people that warmed his heart of old?*
>
> —Charles Dickens

Dickens' Haunted House Party

So many of us grew up with Charles Dickens's *A Christmas Carol*. If you didn't read the book, you've surely seen either the Disney version featuring Scrooge McDuck as Ebenezer Scrooge or one of the countless made-for-TV reenactments. While still true to its Victorian roots, the strong moral about the evils of greed and hoarding are as relevant today as they were then. But what do I (and likely you) like best about this classic? It has ghosts! Ghosts of the past, the present, and the future, a veritable three-card tarot spread of supernatural significance. It is one of the things I most look forward to when the season of bright and shiny presents and happy elves begins to cloy.

Charles Dickens's Christmas ghosts were rampant in his 1894 pamphlet *Christmas Stories*, a holiday

supplement to *All Year Round*, a publication for which Dickens served as editor. *The Haunted House* is both a fictional house where like-minded guests and ghosts gather and a literary gold mine, where Dickens's favorite authors of the day gathered to tell their particularly assigned ghost stories. In other words, Dickens created the setting, and each room of the Haunted House was assigned to one of his favorite writers (and to himself).

The story begins on a train, where our main character is bound for an unnamed town, seeking respite in a residence we come to learn—at least, according to the local townspeople—is haunted. Naturally, he rents it in all of its neglected glory for six months.

He writes:

Under none of the accredited ghostly circumstances, and environed by none of the conventional ghostly surroundings, did I first make acquaintance with the house which is the subject of this Christmas piece. I saw it in the daylight, with the sun upon it. There was no wind, no rain, no lightning, no thunder, no awful or unwonted circumstance, of any kind, to heighten its effect. More than that: I had come to it direct from a railway station: it was not more than a mile distant from the railway station; and, as I stood outside the house, looking back upon the way I had come, I could see the goods train running smoothly along the embankment in the valley. I will not say that everything was utterly commonplace, because I doubt if anything can be that, except to utterly commonplace people—and there my vanity steps in; but, I will take it on myself to say that anybody might see the house as I saw it, any fine autumn morning.

[. . .]

Within, I found it, as I had expected, transcendently dismal. The slowly changing shadows waved on it from the heavy trees, were doleful in the last degree; the house was ill-placed, ill-built, ill-planned, and ill-fitted. It was damp, it was not from dry rot, there was a flavour of rats in it, and it was the gloomy victim of that indescribable decay which settles

> **The slowly changing shadows waved on it from the heavy trees, were doleful in the last degree; the house was ill-placed, ill-built, ill-planned, and ill-fitted.**

on all the work of man's hands whenever it's not turned to man's account. The kitchens and offices were too large, and too remote from each other. Above stairs and below, waste tracts of passage intervened between patches of fertility represented by rooms; and there was a mouldy old well with a green growth upon it, hiding like a murderous trap, near the bottom of the back-stairs, under the double row of bells. One of these bells was labelled, on a black ground in faded white letters, Master B. This, they told me, was the bell that rang the most.

It was a loud, unpleasant bell, and made a very disagreeable sound. The other bells were inscribed according to the names of the rooms to which their wires were conducted: as "Picture Room," "Double Room," "Clock Room," and the like.

Not long after his procuring this house for rent, as our character continues to narrate, the servants seem to go mad with fear. After being unable to keep any servants for more than a week's time and having gone through a few rounds of servants, our main character, who is residing in the home with his somewhat unconventional sister, hatches a new plan. The two decide to keep the house the remaining months without conventional servants (imagine the horror), and instead invite their dearest friends to take up residence.

Dickens writes:

> The first thing we did when we were all
> assembled, was, to draw lots for bedrooms.
> That done, and every bedroom, and, indeed,
> the whole house, having been minutely exam-
> ined by the whole body, we allotted the various
> duties, as if we had been on a gipsy party, or
> a yachting party, or a hunting party, or were
> shipwrecked.

Among the party there was our main character and his sister; their cousin John and his lovely wife; one Alfred Starling, a young, agreeable fellow with a generous, inherited stipend; Ms. Belinda Bates—a poet at the forefront of the woman's liberation movement who, to quote Dickens, "'goes in' for Woman's mission, Woman's rights, Woman's wrongs, and everything that is woman's with a capital W, or is not and ought to be, or is and ought not to be."

Perhaps the liveliest of the characters are the beloved and salty sailor, Jack Governor, who invited along his own pal for the residence, one Nat Beaver, a comrade and merchantman.

Dickens says:

Mr. Beaver, with a thick-set wooden face and figure, and apparently as hard as a block all over, proved to be an intelligent man, with a world of watery experiences in him, and great practical knowledge. At times, there was a curious nervousness about him, apparently the lingering result of some old illness; but, it seldom lasted many minutes. He got the Cupboard Room.

The rules were laid out:

[...]

We [...] gravely called one another to witness, that we were not there to be deceived, or to deceive—which we considered pretty much the same thing—and that, with a serious sense of responsibility, we would be strictly true to one another, and would strictly follow out the truth. The understanding was established, that any one who heard unusual noises in the night, and who wished to trace them, should knock at my door; lastly, that on Twelfth Night, the last night of holy Christmas, all our individual experiences since that then present hour of our coming together in the haunted house, should be brought to light for the good of all; and that we would hold our peace on the subject till then, unless on some remarkable provocation to break silence.

The engagement among us was faithfully kept, and nobody revealed anything.

Dickens published the collection together in *Christmas Stories*. Among the contributors we find George Augustus Henry Sala—a Londoner by birth. Dickens became a fan of Sala's early writings and published both articles and stories by him, including this selection from *The Haunted House*, "The Ghost in the Double Room." Sala later became a regular contributor to the *Daily Telegraph*, and his bombastic style helped set the tone of one of the most prestigious newspapers in the world. He was famous for having the most impressive library in London, having amassed a large collection of books so that he could write on virtually every subject.

"The Ghost in the Picture Room" is channeled by Adelaide Anne Procter. Procter was a poet and philanthropist who died at the young age of thirty-eight in 1864. She was a native Londoner who held the honor of being Queen Victoria's favorite poet. In Procter's time she was considered second only to Alfred Lord Tennyson in poet popularity. Dickens first began publishing Procter in *All Year Round* when she was just a teenager. It is no wonder, then, that the tale of "The Ghost in the Picture Room" is a long, rhyming poem.

Author Elizabeth Gaskell tells the longest of the stories in the collection with "The Ghost in the Garden Room." It paints a vivid portrait of the ghost of a judge. Elizabeth Gaskell was a successful English novelist and short story writer who, like Dickens, was known for writing about the classism in Victorian society. She was most well known for her 1848 novel *Mary Barton*, as well as *North and South* (1855), *Wives and Daughters* (1865), and the first-ever biography of Charlotte Brontë (*The Life of Charlotte Brontë*), which came out in 1857.

Dear Wilkie Collins, born in London in 1824, met Dickens in 1851. Shortly after meeting, both men acted together in Edward "Dark and Stormy Night" Bulwer-Lytton's play *Not So Bad as We Seem*. This set the stage for what would become a lifelong friendship. Like Dickens and most of Victorian England, Collins had a healthy relationship with the idea of ghosts. That is to say, he believed in them—at least as a literary device. He wrote dozens of plays, short stories, and novels, the most famous of which was called *The Woman in White*, which was later adapted for the stage and even modern film. Collins died in 1889 of a stroke. According to Troy Taylor in his book *Field Guide to Haunted Graveyards*, Collins always carried around a letter with instructions to his family to be sure that he did not receive a premature burial. For Dickens's collection, Collins wrote "The Ghost in the Cupboard Room," where we find the aforementioned Nat Beaver, who tells of being haunted but not by a conventional ghost. He is haunted, quite literally, by a candle.

My favorite of the stories is Hesba Stretton's "The Ghost in the Clock Room." Hesba Stretton was the pen name of an English gentlewoman called Sarah Smith. She became a contributor to *All Year Round* when her sister, without Sarah's knowledge, submitted a piece that Dickens accepted for publication. She is most well known for having written a book in 1866 called *Jessica's First Prayer*, which had sold over a million and a half copies by the end of the nineteenth century! She died in 1911.

The Adventurous Victorian World-Traveler

E. Katherine Bates was an Englishwoman of independent means. The daughter of a reverend, her father passed when she was just nine years old, but she writes that he had been ill most of her early years. In the intro-duction to her 1908 book *Seen and Unseen*, she writes about her first psychic experience during the time when her father was dying:

When only nine years old I lost my father—the Rev. John Ellison Bates of Christ Church, Dover—and my earliest childish experience of anything supernormal was connected with him. He had been an invalid all my short life, and I was quite accustomed to spending days at a time without seeing him. His last illness, which lasted about a fortnight, had therefore no special significance for me, and my nurse, elder brother, and godmother, who were the only three people in the house at the time, gave strict orders that none of the servants should give me a hint of his being dangerously ill. These instructions were carefully carried out, and yet I dreamed three nights running—the three nights preceding his decease—that he was dead. I was entirely devoted to my father, who had been father and mother to me in one, and these dreams no doubt broke the terrible shock of his death to me. How well I remember, that cold, dreary February morning, being hastily dressed by candle-light by strange hands, and then my dear old nurse (who had been by his bedside all night) coming in and telling me the sad news with tears streaming down her cheeks. It seemed no news at the moment; and yet I had spoken of my dreams to no one, "for fear they should come true," having some pathetic, childish notion that silence on my part might avert the catastrophe. In all his previous and numerous illnesses I had never dreamt that any special one was fatal.

In her early adult years she spent time with Morton, the grandson of her godfather whom she describes as a "very good sensitive." In fact, she and Morton together "could move a heavy dining-room table, or any other piece of heavy furniture quite beyond our normal powers, practically without exerting any strength at all."

Bates traveled the world in pursuit of the psychic arts, which was almost unheard of at the time for anyone, let alone a young woman! She visited the United States in

1885 and again seven years later, conducting psychic investigations, sitting in on séances in paranormal parlors, developing her own clairvoyant confidence, and sometimes acting as a medium herself. In 1887, she sailed for Australia and New Zealand, where her first experience involved channeling the ghost of George Eliot. She soon set sail again in 1888 for Hong Kong, Alaska, and back to New York, and in 1890 she traveled with a friend to India. Two years later she pressed on to Russia and Sweden, Egypt, Italy, and beyond. She was particularly intrigued by something called psychometry. She writes:

In the interests of non-psychic readers, I may explain that psychometry is the science of learning to receive impressions and intuitions from the atmosphere surrounding any material object—a letter, a ring, a piece of pebble or shell, and so naturally this is especially the case in letters written and signed by us.

A handy skill to have for a world traveler, Bates became rather adept at this art. I would be lying if I said I did not have a particular affinity for this woman and her remarkable pursuits. It seems, at least from her writing, that not only was she open-minded about the spirit realm but also open to the ways and subtleties of other cultures. In addition, she not only spent time attending psychic salons but all the while learned to truly trust her own intuition. In the book *Seen and Unseen* she takes us back to a haunted castle in Ireland. In it, she makes reference to Mr. W. T. Stead. William Thomas Stead was a known Spiritualist but was also a controversial and radical newspaper publisher and writer who was best known during his life for his support of what was later called the Stead

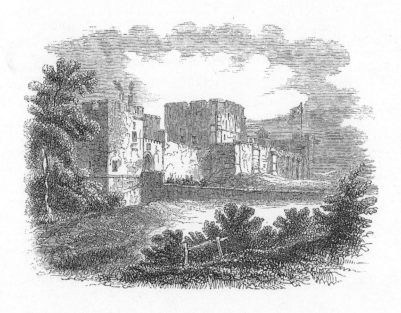

Act: raising the consent of marriage to a young girl from thirteen to sixteen. Stead also drowned on the *Titanic*. And on that note, on to the next chapter.

> *Think you're escaping and run into yourself.*
> *Longest way round is the shortest way home.*
>
> —JAMES JOYCE

Chapter 5

Belly Up to the Bar

Burial Traditions and Customs,
Funeral Food and Drink, and Other
Fascinating Facts Associated with Death

Out—out are the lights—out all:
  And over each quivering form,
The curtain, a funeral pall,
  Comes down with the rush of a storm—
And the angels, all pallid and wan,
  Uprising, unveiling, affirm
That the play is the tragedy, "Man,"
  And its hero, the conqueror Worm.

—EDGAR ALLAN POE, *LIGEIA*

Giving Up the Ghosts

You can't very well undertake a book about ghosts without exploring the topic of death. Few subjects fascinate and terrify us, perhaps even terrorize us, like the subject of death. We fear the loss of life, and yet we are perpetually fascinated with the prospects. We can scarcely tear ourselves away from the gruesome details of the latest serial killer's methods; we pour money into shows that tangle with life after death. And yet, when faced with the prospect of our own, we have been known to cower in fear and negotiate our firstborn child. (The royal "we," of course.)

Furthermore, we spend countless hours detailing our last will and testament, lest Auntie Jackie make off with all of Grandma Bean's money. While the subject of death customs and funeral rites could clearly make up a volume of work on its own (hmm . . . cogs turning), I offer you here just a smattering of some of the more fascinating tidbits when it comes to practices, customs, traditions, lore, and superstitions surrounding the inevitable dance with the Grim Reaper.

Give me that old soft shoe . . .

What Not to Wear

The custom of dressing somberly and in black is not as strictly adhered to today as it was in Victorian times; in Western culture there was a great deal of etiquette that went along with funeral garb. While the lower classes or servants were allowed to wear somber clothing of a dark nature (but not necessarily strictly black), members of the middle and upper crusts of society were expected to wear modest, plain, and appropriately black attire. According to Deborah Noyes in her book *The Encyclopedia of the End*, the tradition of what to wear to a funeral was taken so gravely in Victorian times that it gave rise to massive stores dedicated just to that purpose. She writes:

> Mourning warehouses—what the French call *maisons de noir*—were actually the first department stores. . . . All but the most destitute, it was understood, should follow a particular code of dress—even small children. . . . Mourning houses began to appear in the 1840s to satisfy the clamor for "black goods," and the bigger houses, such as Grande Maison de Noir in Paris, or the House of Jay in London, offered true one-stop shopping for the bereaved. That is, everything from a hearse to an etiquette book to guide your household through the process.

In parts of China, only the spouse, children, and daughters-in-law dress in black. Grandchildren wear dark blue and great-grandchildren, siblings, cousins, aunts, uncles, and so on may also wear blue. In other parts of the country, the immediate family must wear white and others must wear bright colors at the funeral. Most often, somber colors are used for the death of younger people, but if the deceased was elderly, typically over eighty, bright colors may be encouraged, as it is considered a celebration of life. In most cases, red is discouraged. Traditional Hindu funerals call for white garb for the grieving friends and family, and formal black attire is actually considered impolite.

I'm Not Dead Yet

The fear of being buried alive still takes its place in the top ten list of "the worst thing imaginable," but the truth is, it used to happen with alarming frequency. There are terrifying accounts of bodies found outside their coffins or crypts, hands bloodied from the attempt to get out, and of unsuspecting grave robbers discovering the inside of coffins wretched with scratch marks. Even as recently as 2005, a funeral director in Massachusetts found a corpse in a body bag to actually be alive. In 2014, a

> **The fear of being buried alive still takes its place in the top ten list of "the worst thing imaginable," but the truth is, it used to happen with alarming frequency.**

woman in Macedonia was reported as having been buried alive: children playing near the cemetery could hear her screams. She was dug up but died of asphyxia shortly after being transported to the hospital. A 2015  case in Greece was quite similar: when visiting the grave of the deceased, the family claimed to hear her screams. Upon exhuming the body and conducting an autopsy, it was found that she had died in the coffin of a heart attack and had appeared dead prior because of a medically induced coma.

Prevention of premature burial led to the invention of "safety coffins" as well as various devices to allow buried people to summon help: a pipe that could provide air into the coffin, a safety hatch built into a vault, and even a glass pane in the coffin, which was laid out in a mausoleum. Passersby could check to see if the glass had been breathed on or any signs of life were contained within.

Ding Dong, You're Wrong

Throughout Great Britain, it was once customary for the sexton—the traditional keeper of the churchyard and cemetery and often also the grave digger—to walk the town's streets ringing his little bell and announcing a person's death. He would also give the time and date of the funeral. It is also believed that the bell, when made of silver or brass especially, could ward off evil and assure safe passage for the deceased, and the sexton traditionally would also walk at the head of the funeral procession, ringing the bell. In ancient times the bell would be rung when someone was dying, in order to keep the untoward spirits from claiming the soon-to-be-departed's soul. Traditional Chinese funerals also include the ringing of bells during the service and at the grave.

Slowly She Crept

The word *hearse* has taken several linguistic turns from its origins in 51 BC to its usage in sixteenth-century England to modern times. In ancient Rome a farmer would plow his fields and then use a tool known as a *hirpex* to rake the land. Conquering western Europe, the Romans introduced this agricultural tool to their new subjects, and the tool became commonly called a *harrow* in the British Isles. When the Normans invaded England they called the harrow a *herse*. They also began the practice of inverting the herse, as it bore resemblance to their own ecclesiastical candelabras. In time, all church candelabras became known as herses, and they grew in size. The candelabras were a common part of a funeral ceremony, beginning the association of a herse with a funeral. In time, the herse itself rested on the coffin as the funeral procession made its way to the burial grounds. (The funeral procession needed to move slowly, lest the herse's candles blow out, and the tradition of slow-moving funeral processions continues today.) By the next century, the entire cart that carried the coffin became known as the *hearse*.

—VARLA VENTURA, *BEYOND BIZARRE*

Time drops in decay
Like a candle burnt out.
And the mountains and woods
Have their day, have their day;
But, kindly old rout
Of the fire-born moods,
You pass not away.

—W. B. YEATS

Oh, Man That's an Omen: Corpse Candles and Death Birds

There is a death omen in Wales that is not the fearsome banshee or warning ghost popular in the folklore of British Isles. The Canwyll Corph, aka the Corpse Candle, is the appearance of a disembodied candle with a ghastly blue flame or the appearance of a ghost holding a candle. When inspected closely (if possible), the ghost may take on the form of someone living: this is the doomed person who will soon die. The size of the candle has significance also: a small candle can indicate an infant or child, a larger one indicates an adult, and two candles together can often be a mother and child. Also popular in Welsh folklore is the Aderyn y Corph, a bird that chirps at the door of a person who will soon die.

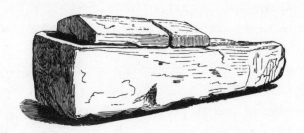

Coffin Door

Ever noticed those extra wide doors on historic homes? According to one docent at the historic Fillebrown House in White Bear Lake, Minnesota, the doors are referred to as "coffin doors" because back in the 1800s it was customary for pivotal figures in a town to host funerals or wakes in their homes. The extra-wide door allowed for the casket to more easily come and go.

Gone But Not Forgotten

From 1900–1910, J. Maxwell Wood was the editor and publisher of *The Gollovidian*—an illustrated magazine in Galloway, Scotland, that ran from 1899 to 1949. He was said to be a dentist and also wrote two books, *Smuggling the Soloway and Around the Galloway Sea-board* and *Witchcraft and Superstitious Record in the South-Western District of Scotland*. In the latter, he claimed he observed a number of specific Scottish customs during and just after the death of a household member. Those customs include the following:

The nearest relative bent down to the dying face to receive the last breath. (Perhaps this is where we get the expression, "takes my breath away.")

The door should be kept ajar, although not too wide that the spirit might be untrammelled in its flight.

The spirit flees before the poor dead eyes were closed, so keep copper coins to be place upon them.

The looking glass in the death-chamber was covered with a white cloth.

The clock was stopped or at least the striking-weight removed.

Daily routines and work discontinued for several days. These "dead days" meant there could be no plowing, seed sowing, or even harvest.

Dogs and cats were kept from the house and sometimes imprisoned to keep them in one place, because it was believed that if either of these animals crossed over the body the deceased spirit's welfare could be affected.

The body is washed and dressed and the hands of females crossed over the breast, the hands of males extended by the sides. Last of all a plate of salt was placed upon the breast. This was either because it signified future life or because it had the practical application of keeping swelling down.

In Scotland, Wales, and Ireland a once-common funeral practice was the act of "sin-eating." A piece of bread is placed upon the salt by someone who has been previously designated as the "sin eater." The sin-eater would eat the bread, therefore absolving the dead of their sins. This was sometimes a paid position. The Scottish term "dishaloof" comes from this custom but may also refer to the placing of plates in three places on the body or sometimes on the hearth. The Welsh, too, practiced sin-eating, and there are even examples of sin-eating as a profession. This person was sent for at the appropriate time to eat the bread from the dish of salt upon the breast of the corpse, but unfortunately for the sin-eater, he was often shunned by regular society and lived a somewhat reclusive and admonished life, as it was believed that he took up the sins into his own life. Occasionally in place of bread and salt you will find accounts of an apple or orange quartered and laid upon the body, which the sin-eater was expected to consume.

For ancient Romans, burial was of the utmost importance. According to Harold Whetston Johnston's book *The Private Life of Romans*, it was fiercely believed that the soul would not be at rest until the body was in the ground. In the cases of bodies lost at sea, the Romans would often erect tombs in their honor. If for any reason the body could not be interred, scattering three handfuls of dust over the body was sufficient for the happiness of the spirit. Later, when cremation became more common, it was still believed that the ashes or remains must be buried in the earth. Often, a lingering finger bone or toe bone would do. Originally, the head of the household was actually buried underneath the hearthstone in his house. Later, the custom was to bury him in the garden until eventually this practice was outlawed. The Romans also had "burial societies" to oversee the funeral expenses of other members of the society: you paid your dues, and this insured your body would be treated correctly after you died.

Not unlike the tradition in Scotland of leaning over for the last breath, if a Roman died at home it was the duty of his oldest son to bend over the body and call out the dying man's name, hoping to restore life. Sometimes a person might lean over the corpse as if in a kiss to steal that dying breath. When (of course) this did not happen, the son would say, *"conclāmātum est,"* which means "it is given up for lost." The eyes were closed, the body was anointed, and if the deceased was an officer in the government or military, a death mask would be taken (this is literally a paraffin wax impression of the deceased's face). No coins were placed over eyes, but in early Rome a coin was put on the mouth: the fee for the passage across the River Styx. The body was then laid out on a funeral couch (feet to the door), flowers were strewn about it, and incense was burned. Above the door boughs of pine or cypress were set to warn of death.

In China and Chinese tradition, mirrors are removed immediately following the death of a family member. Statues and figurines of religious importance are covered with red paper or cloth. The doorway is outfitted with a white cloth and gongs on either side.

Spade Money

Before undertaking their task, gravediggers
once held out their spades for mourners to toss
coins into. If you didn't make your offering,
he might "shake his spade at you," which was
considered a curse of bad luck or illness.

The Walking Dead

In rural Scotland there was once a custom that, after
the body had been washed and dressed, friends and
neighbors would express sympathies by sitting with
the body, not unlike a wake. By
watching, or "waulking," the
dead all through the long hours
of the night (often by candle-
light), they could be sure that
the person was indeed dead. It
was also believed that touching the corpse would help prevent illness, disease, and creepy
dreams.

> It was also
> believed that
> touching the
> corpse would
> help prevent
> illness, disease,
> and creepy
> dreams.

So Long, Farewell

Sul Coffa is the old Welsh custom of honoring the dead on the first Sunday after the funeral as well as every Sunday thereafter until grief has sufficiently subsided. The word *keening*—the wailing sound made when mourning, which can sometimes take on a songlike melody—is derived from the Irish word *caoinim,* meaning "I wail." The mournful cry of the banshee is thought to be similar, as some believe the banshee is a trapped spirit, frozen in grief and doomed to wander the countryside looking for her dead child or loved one and warning those who can hear her that death is nigh. It was once a custom in Ireland to continue mourning after death and to sometimes dig up skulls to howl over.

Are You Going to Eat That?
Funeral Food and Drink

In William Wirt Sikes's *British Goblins*, his chapter "Sponge Cake at Funerals" discusses the traditional Welsh funerals. I can see him perhaps sneaking into the back row of church pews to eavesdrop on the funeral customs of the local townsfolk.

His affinity for the Welsh people and their festive spirit is perhaps clearest in this passage:

> When an Englishman is drunk he is belligerent; when a Frenchman is drunk he is amorous; when an Italian is drunk he is loquacious; when a Scotchman is drunk he is argumentative; when a German is drunk he is sleepy; when an American is drunk he brags; and when a Welshman is drunk he sings. Sometimes he dances.

And what of these sponge cakes? It was custom for the upper class to have sponge cakes baked, small and oblong in form, and wrapped in paper. These were distributed across the coffin to funeral-goers. The funeral director kept these little cakes in his pockets and directly on the coffin, sometimes with other food and drink. Sometimes this duty fell to the family. Sikes writes:

> After taking the coffin out of the house and placing it on a bier near the door, it was formerly customary for one of the relatives of the deceased to distribute bread and cheese to the poor, taking care to hand it to each one over the coffin. These poor people were usually those who had, in expectation of this gift, been busily engaged in gathering flowers and herbs with which to grace the coffin. Sometimes this dole was supplemented by the gift of a loaf of bread or a cheese with a piece of money placed inside it. After that a cup of drink was presented, and

the receiver was required to drink a little of it immediately.

In olde Scotland the following list was standard service for a funeral spread:

Bread and cheese, with ale and porter
Whisky, with bread and cheese
Rum and biscuits
Brandy and a currant bun
Wine and shortbread

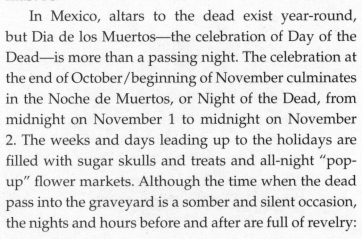

Not surprisingly, funeral expenses could get quite high with all of that liquor, but oh, what a consolation it must be.

In Mexico, altars to the dead exist year-round, but Dia de los Muertos—the celebration of Day of the Dead—is more than a passing night. The celebration at the end of October/beginning of November culminates in the Noche de Muertos, or Night of the Dead, from midnight on November 1 to midnight on November 2. The weeks and days leading up to the holidays are filled with sugar skulls and treats and all-night "pop-up" flower markets. Although the time when the dead pass into the graveyard is a somber and silent occasion, the nights and hours before and after are full of revelry:

Although the time when the dead pass into the graveyard is a somber and silent occasion, the nights and hours before and after are full of revelry.

drinking, building floral displays, and remembering. Entire families camp out in the graveyards and work together to honor their beloved departed. November 1 is typically a night to honor children and those who are lost souls. The following evening is in honor of all the dead, and it is believed especially powerful to make offerings to anyone who has passed on in the last year. Special breads called *pan de muerto* are baked and consumed graveside or placed on

altars, tied to the headstones and flower arrangements. Meals including the dead's favorite soups and stews are laid out on altars. Sugar skulls are sometimes eaten but most often used as a decoration and can come in the form of skulls, skeletons, coffins, hearts, and more.

Herbs of Death: A Brief Survey

There are hundreds of plants used in rituals from body cleansing to ceremonial incense to lining graves from cultures around the world. Here are just a few examples.

Cypress is thought to help communicate with the dead. The essential oil can be applied (sparingly) to the third eye. In Scott Cunningham's *Magical Herbalism*, he refers to cypress as the "Tree of Death."

Any plant associated with Saturn may be traditionally used in funeral and death rites. Saturn—the Roman god of karma and patience—is the equivalent to the Greek Kronos, the god of time. Both are sometimes depicted as Father Time. Herbs associated with Saturn include many that have powerful scents—suggesting that memory and scent can connect us to time and the past—including dill, garlic, valerian, and the very fragrant asafetida.

Pluto, the controversial questioned planet (is that just a big star or are you happy to see me?), is strongly associated with death, regeneration, and rebirth in magical workings. Herbs that fall under Pluto's domain include many psychotropic plants such as fly agaric, wormwood, and psilocybin. (Go figure.)

Hemlock is associated with death, perhaps because of its extremely lethal qualities. Socrates committed suicide by drinking a concoction made from the poison.

According to Mary Sissip Geniusz's book of Anishinaabe botanical teachings, *Plants Have So Much to Give Us, All We Have to Do Is Ask*, cedar mats were used to line graves. The Anishinaabe refer to death as "passing over," and as Grandmother Cedar provides so much in life—from a medicinal tea high in vitamin C and soothing of stomach ailments to cedar rope to moldretarding cedar bags for leather and food goods—it is no wonder

Grandmother Cedar is trusted in graves.

"The Passing Over Place" is the traditional name for the grave because that is the place where one "passes over to the Sprit World." It is also called the "Paying Back Place" because it is there that a person has the opportunity to repay the Earth for all the sustenance that has been given that person throughout his or her lifetime. In the traditional society cedar mats were used to line graves, so that a person might finish their life as they had begun it and lived it, surrounded by Grandmother Cedar.

Ancient Egyptians burned myrrh, the pleasant scent of which was thought to appease the gods. Queen Hatshepshut sent her navy on a botanical mission to the Land of Punt (which is thought to be in northeast Africa) and made a swap: bangles, jewels, and tools for sacks of myrrh and other goods, including thirty-one fresh myrrh saplings. The queen was so thrilled by the beautiful plants she had them depicted in relief on the temple walls of her future tomb.

Foxglove, *Digitalis purpurea*, is also referred to as Deadman's Bells. Although foxglove produces the single most powerful drug to prevent heart failure, chewing the leaves can cause sudden paralysis and heart failure.

It was once customary in Wales to plant rue, thistles, nettles, and henbane on the graves of old bachelors. In contrast to the practice of planting white roses on the grave of a young woman, the thistles and weed-like plants signified the unpleasantness of lifelong bachelorhood. It was also common to strew the grave of a young unmarried person with evergreens and sweet-scented flowers.

> *O Earth! O Earth! Observe this well*
> *That earth to earth must come to dwell*
> *Then earth in earth shall close remain,*
> *Till earth from earth shall rise again.*

> —Epitaph on the grave of Edward Morgan,
> Gla'norganshire, W. H. Howe,
> *Everybody's Book of Epitaphs*

Just remember, my darlings, death is not the end.

THE END

Bibliography

Anonymous. "They Tried to Call Up Spirits." *Sacramento Daily Union*, Vol. 95, No. 146, July 1898. Accessed via the California Digital Newspaper Collection online archives, March 4, 2017. *cdnc.ucr.edu/cgibin/cdnc?a=d&d=SDU18980717.2.59.*

Buckland, Raymond. *The Weiser Field Guide to Ghosts.* San Francisco: Red Wheel/Weiser, 2009.

Chappell, Vere. *Sexual Outlaw, Erotic Mystic: The Essential Ida Craddock.* San Francisco: Red Wheel/Weiser, 2010.

Cunningham, Scott. *Magical Herbalism.* St. Paul: Llewellyn Publications, 1996.

Dalby, Richard, ed. *The Mammoth Book of Victorian & Edwardian Ghost Stories.* New York: Carroll & Graf Publishers, Inc., 1995.

Diliberto, Gioia. "Patience Worth, Author from the Great Beyond," *Smithsonian Magazine*, September 2010, *www.smithsonianmag.com/arts-culture/patience-worth-author-from-the-great-beyond-54333749/*.

Geniusz, Mary Siisip. *Plants Have So Much to Give Us, All We Have to Do Is Ask: Anishinaabe Botanical Teachings*. Minneapolis: University of Minnesota Press, 2015.

Guetebier, Amber and Brenda Knight. *The Poetry Oracle*. San Francisco: CCC Publishing, 2008.

Hall, Joan Wylie. "White mamma . . . black mammy: Replacing the Absent Mother in the Works of Ruth McEnery Stuart" from *Southern Mothers: Fact and Fictions in Southern Women's Writing*. New Orleans: LSU Press, 1999.

Harrison, Karen. *The Herbal Alchemist Handbook*. San Francisco: Red Wheel/Weiser, 2011.

Holzer, Hans. *The Lively Ghosts of Ireland*. New York: Ace Books, 1967.

Howe, W. H. *Everybody's Book of Epitaphs*. Whitstable, England: Pryor Publications, 1995.

Leek, Sybil. *Sybil Leek's Book of the Curious and the Occult*. New York: Ballantine, 1976.

Leodhas, Nic Sorche. *Ghost Go Haunting*. New York: Holt, Reinhart and Winston, 1965.

Mary, Bloody. *Bloody Mary's Guide to Hauntings, Horrors, and Dancing with the Dead*. San Francisco: Red Wheel/Weiser, 2016.

Morris, Jeff, Garett Merk, and Dain Charbonneau. *Twin Cities Haunted Handbook*. St. Paul: Clerisy Press: 2011.

Noyes, Deborah. *Encyclopedia of the End*. Boston: Houghton Mifflin, 2008.

Pipenberg, Dan. "Shades of Mark Twain," *The Paris Review* blog, March 4, 2016. *www.theparisreview.org/blog/tag/emily-grant-hutchings/*.

Plath, Sylvia. *Ariel: The Restored Edition*. New York: Harper Collins, 2004.

——. *The Journals of Sylvia Plath*. New York: Dial Press, 1982.

Pramis, Joshua. "Hotels Haunted by Celebrities," *Travel and Leisure*, October 5, 2015, *www.travelandleisure.com/slideshows/hotels-haunted-by-celebrities*.

Reader's Digest. *Plants in Myth and Magic*. New York: Readers Digest Association, Inc., 2006.

Spence, Lewis. *An Encyclopedia of Occultism*. New York: University Books, 1968.

Stockwell, Kallene. *Haunted Nevada: Gold Hill Hotel and Miners Cabin*. Channel 2 News, KTVU, Oct. 29, 2008. *www.ktvn.com/story/9263016/haunted-nevada-gold-hill-hotel-and-miners-cabin*.

Taylor, Troy. *Field Guide to Haunted Graveyards*. Alton, IL: Whitechapel Productions Press, 2003.

Ventura, Varla. *The Book of the Bizarre: Freaky Facts and Strange Stories*. San Francisco: Red Wheel/Weiser, 2008.

——. *Beyond Bizarre: Frightening Facts and Blood Curdling True Tales*. San Francisco: Red Wheel/Weiser, 2010.

——. *Banshees, Werewolves, Vampires and Other Creatures of the Night*. San Francisco: Red Wheel/Weiser, 2013.

———. *Fairies, Pookas, and Changelings: A Complete Guide to the Wild and Wicked Enchanted Realm*. Newburyport, MA: Red Wheel/Weiser, 2017.

Willson, Beckles. *Occultism and Common-Sense*. London: T. Werner Laurie, publication date unknown. *www.gutenberg.org/files/36730/36730-h/36730-h .htm#CHAPTER_IV.*

Wolfgram, Christian. "Doom and Board: Four Ghost Stories from LA's Most Famous Haunted Hotels." From *LA Magazine*, online edition, published Oct. 5, 2015. Accessed on 1/15/17; *www.lamag.com/culturefiles/ doom-and-board-four-ghost-stories-from-l-a-s-most-famous- haunted-hotels/.*

Websites

hauntedhouses.com
hauntedrooms.com
legendsofamerica.com
maplewoodmn.gov/1621/Ramsey-County-Poor-Farm
maplewoodmn.gov/1622/The-Ramsey-County-Poor-Farm- Cemetery
northhamptonstatehospital.org
prabook.com/web/person-view.html?profileId=1090170
prestoncastle.com
ramseycounty.us
therealwaverlyhills.com
silverqueenhotel.net

travelchannel.com/shows/ghost-adventures/episodes/crazy-town#episode-tunein

travelchannel.com/shows/ghost-adventures/episodes/crazy-town

Via Gutenberg.Org

Bates, E. Katherine. *Seen and Unseen*. New York: Dodge Publishing, 1908.

Holland, Bob. W., ed. *Twenty-Five Ghost Stories*. New York: J.S. Oglivie Publishing Company, 1904.

Johnston, Harold Whetstone. *The Private Life of Romans*. Chicago: Forseman and Company, 1909.

MacKay, Charles. *Memoirs of Extraordinary Popular Delusions and the Madness of Crowds*. London: Office of the National Illustrated Library, 1852.

Merivale, Charles Herman. *My Experiences in a Lunatic Asylum*. London: Chatto and Windus, 1879.

O'Donnell, Elliott. *Some Haunted Houses of England & Wales*. London: Fawside House, 1908.

Wood, J. Maxwell. *Superstitious Record in the South-Western District of Scotland*. Dumfries, Scotland: J. Maxwell & Son, 1911.

Acknowledgments

To the ghosts of Victoria and Carlo Martucci, Henry Guetebier, Sybil Leek, Espi Petterson, Phillip Poblete, Raymond Buckland, Jim Warner, and Meg Richardson—without you these stories would not, could not, be here.

To my wonderful family, who is ever supportive, especially my witchy and wonderful mother, Dolores. And to all of my spooky-ooky friends who burn the midnight oil with me night after night. All ye pirates, sinners, and saints.

A big gracious thank you to my contributors: Dave Cruz, Chris Ward, Ron Kolek, Jeff Belanger,

Joe Diamond, Alix Benedict, Hunter Shea, and Bo Luellen. Thanks also to Annetta Black and the whole Odd Salon crew for their support.

To the staff at Weiser Books, especially Judika Illes, Jane Hagaman, Michael Kerber, Eryn Eaton, Bonni Hamilton, Sylvia Hopkins, and Mike Conlon.

And to you, dear reader, for wandering library halls and bookstores, touching spirit boards and recording EVPs—may you always find a ghost story you love.